TOUGH COOKIE

TOUGH COOKIE

Sheila Mottley

Hodder & Stoughton

LONDON SYDNEY AUCKLAND TORONTO

British Library Cataloguing-in-Publication Data

Mottley, Sheila
  Tough cookie.
  I. Title
  920

  ISBN 0-340-55833-4

First published in Great Britain 1991

Published by Hodder and Stoughton,
a division of Hodder and Stoughton Ltd,
Mill Road, Dunton Green, Sevenoaks, Kent TN13 2YA.
Editorial Office: 47 Bedford Square, London WC1B 3DP.

Photoset by E.P.L. BookSet, Norwood, London.

Printed in Great Britain by T.J. Press (Padstow) Ltd,
Padstow, Cornwall.

To my four children
I hope this brings us closer together

Contents

Acknowledgments

The author and publishers would like to thank the following for allowing them to reproduce copyright material:

the *Daily Mirror* for the photographs of Janette at Marple Children's Home; the *News of the World* for the article featuring Janette on her tenth birthday; *Manchester Evening News* for the photographs of Sheila with Kelli-Anne; Janette with Kelli-Anne and Sheila, Bob and Janette with Kelli-Anne; *The Sunday Times* for the photograph of Kelli-Anne being fed by Janette.

I would like to give my special thanks to Jenny Cuffe and Keiren Phelan. Without these two wonderful people this book would not have been possible.

PREFACE

In November 1961 I was twenty, pregnant for the third time after losing two previous babies at birth, and reluctantly married to my Teddy boy lover, Terry. My adoptive parents were appalled at my unruliness and I was knackered from morning sickness. My family doctor in Manchester then prescribed a tranquillizer called Distaval to cure the morning sickness. It did the trick all right. One tablet a day was enough to stop me feeling sick. But things didn't usually work out so well for me and I should have spotted a problem straightaway! In fact that small brown bottle of white pills was to give birth to a whole range of problems which dominated the next thirty years of my life.

Even before I was given the tablets there had been stories in the medical press about the hideous side-effects of Distaval. That was the trade name for thalidomide – a supposedly non-toxic and completely safe drug invented by the German company Chemie Grünenthal. Across the world, thousands of babies had already been born with severe and distinctive deformities and the one thing that appeared to link them together was that their mothers had taken this drug. A few weeks after I cheerfully started swallowing those tablets, thalidomide was grudgingly withdrawn from the British market by the Distillers drinks company which marketed it.

My daughter Janette is one of about eight thousand children in forty-six countries whose lives were twisted and wrecked by a drug which in some countries could be bought over the chemist's counter. It was commonly prescribed to women in the first three months of their pregnancy when the baby's limbs are being formed in the womb. My Janette was born without arms or legs. She just has little flipper-like feet.

Other children had missing limbs, or internal injuries, some were deaf or blind and many died at birth. But most of them had perfectly normal intelligence and I've often said that what Janette lacks in limbs she makes up for in brains and sheer bloody-minded determination.

This book isn't another account of a mother's long-suffering struggle for her disabled child and that child's triumph over disability. Janette has triumphed and I have suffered and struggled, but not in the way you'd expect and not heroically. I wasn't at the forefront of the campaign against Distillers, although I did my bit eventually, and most of the other thalidomide parents didn't want to know me – a one-time prostitute with a black lover and children of mixed race.

The reason I've written this book is because there are things I need to explain for the sake of all my family and for other families who may be in a similar position. I was hopelessly inexperienced when I had Janette, with a husband of twenty-one who worked in a tripe factory and who was completely unable to cope with the enormity of what had happened. I probably made many mistakes but I always did my best for Janette and for her younger brothers and sister and I always loved them. What's gone wrong with our lives as a family is not just the result of a drug. It's the result of other people's reactions to a disabled child, the way she was made the centre of attention and the jealousies this caused. The money we eventually received in compensation gave us a degree of security and comfort we'd never even dreamt of but it was also one of our biggest problems.

A disabled child dominates the lives of everyone around her. How can you look at a child who's confined to a wheelchair without wanting to make up in every way you can for what she's missing? Janette has told me that, until she was sixteen years old, she thought of her disability as a way of getting whatever she wanted. She soon got used to the fact that passers-by stared and whispered when they saw her. Perhaps the pain of that was worthwhile if it meant she came home to new toys and treats. As she got older she was the centre of attention. The local church and different charities were always taking her on outings. Press photographers would snap up her beaming smile. A special appeal fund set up for thalidomide children helped pay for clothes and holidays. That was lovely for her and I was always glad to see her enjoying things that many children take for granted. But for her brothers, Neil and Karl, and her sister Hayley it was often unbearable. They were never invited to the charity balls. They were shown out of the room while newspaper reporters interviewed Janette. And the money Janette received made her the only rich person in a working-class household.

If I had my time again I'd insist that the other children were included in everything that was organised for their sister. I'd have them all treated equally. But as it is, my able-bodied children have grown up bitter and resentful. All I want is for them to be in one room with no squabbles and no bitchy remarks, but at the moment that's the last thing on their minds. I'm not sure it will ever be possible, but one of my hopes is that this book may help heal the old wounds.

Thalidomide is only one of several nasty thunderbolts in my life. God's certainly chucked at me more than my fair share, maybe because He thinks I can take it. But coping with the effects of thalidomide has shown me how to be tough and it's taught Janette the same. Whatever she's set out to do, she's always succeeded. When she was born, the doctors told me she was unlikely to live long and that she'd never learn to talk or do any of the things other children did. But Janette was talking and reading earlier than most toddlers and at sixteen she went on to a college of further education. None of us ever even thought that she'd become a mother, but in 1986 she made medical history by giving birth to a baby of her own. Kelli-Anne, my granddaughter, is the first baby born to a mother who hasn't any arms or legs, and she's perfect. She's also a chip off the old block, with the same gutsy determination as her mum, and like me she likes life too much for things ever to be calm.

Chapter 1

CAUGHT OUT

My mother handed me over to my adoptive parents for the price of a pair of red shoes. She was a teenager living in Hulme with her mum who was very strict and horrified to learn that an illegitimate grandchild was on its way. From the moment of my birth, on 22nd June 1941, I was marked down for adoption by a couple who'd been waiting for two years. I was led to believe that my natural father was a brave sea captain but much later I discovered he was an Italian prisoner of war, called Ricardo Edmunson.

My adoptive mother really wanted a little boy, to replace the baby she'd lost some years earlier, but when the welfare told her I'd been born she rushed along to the office in Manchester Town Hall to have a look at me. I was only a few weeks old but she made up her mind there and then to take me home. She couldn't contact her husband because he was at work, and she was so frightened someone else might snap me up that she signed the adoption papers and brought me home on the afternoon bus to Levenshulme. On the way to this fairly smart part of Manchester where I was to grow up, mum was so excited she overshot her stop by half a mile and had to walk back to their house in Gordon Avenue.

I came as a complete surprise to my dad when he got home from work that night. To get on the waiting list for adoption you had to have the baby things all ready and waiting so he walked in to find me plumped in the middle of a huge Silver Cross pram in the front room.

There was a six-month waiting period before I could be legally adopted. During that time my natural mother had the chance to change her mind but they heard nothing from her till the morning they were due to meet her in court to

complete the adoption procedure. There she was on the doorstep, a slip of a girl, according to my dad, without proper shoes
on her feet. She wanted to know how much time she had
before the court hearing, and he gave her the money to buy a
pair of shoes. She wore them in court – a pair of red shoes –
and she made no objection to the adoption. All she asked was
that I be brought up as a Roman Catholic.

I had been known as Pauline but mum and dad re-named
me Sheila and they spoiled me from the word go. I was the
only child in the neighbourhood to have a Mickey Mouse gas
mask, which I kept in a little brown case. Fortunately I never
had to use it. In fact the war didn't make much of an impression on me, though I remember the night the Germans
bombed dad's factory, Fairey Aviation, because the next day
the streets were full of shrapnel. Whenever there was an air-
raid, dad would carry me into the Anderson shelter in my
baby bath and then go back for his box of insurance papers.
The shelter was at the bottom of our garden and we shared it
with neighbours who always filled it with the smell of pickled
onions. When the war was over I furnished it and it became
my den.

Mum and dad told me I was adopted when I was five years
old and about to start school. That was quite brave of them,
because lots of people didn't tell their kids things like that. I
don't remember it making much difference to me, and I'm
glad they did tell me. Not long afterwards, one of my new
school-friends bounced up to me in the playground to inform
me of this fact. If she'd hoped to shake my confidence she
must have been disappointed. "I'm luckier than you are!" I
snapped. "Your mum and dad didn't have any choice when
they had you, but my mum and dad had lots of boys and girls
to chose from, and they picked me!" What I lacked in stature
– I was always the smallest kid in the class – I made up for in
other ways and speaking up for myself was one of them. I
remember my dad telling me off for whingeing because a
playmate had thumped me and saying that I had to fight my
own battles in life, and it was a lesson I took on board. I'd
inherited my Italian father's stocky build and maybe my fiery
temper was his doing as well.

Perhaps it was because they'd waited for me and chosen me that my adoptive parents treated me as if I was very special. I was the only child in the school who wasn't allowed to drink my playtime milk cold from the bottle. My mother used to fetch my third of a pint in the morning, heat it and bring it back at eleven o'clock in a brown jug with a cup to drink from. I'd have to wait for her at the school gates and it was a constant embarrassment.

The other daily ritual was the business of taking last night's rags out of my hair and tying it with ribbons. My hair was thick and wavy and mum spent hours brushing and adorning it. Because you couldn't get real ribbons in the war, she used to make her own by melting down pieces of plastic. I don't know what daft magazine she got the idea from but every morning she'd fetch a strip of plastic to match the colour of my dress, then put it on the fireguard till it was soft enough to tie in my hair. If it wasn't dead centre, it had to be taken out and the whole thing done again. Come the evening, the solidified plastic ribbon had to be wrenched from my head before she lovingly brushed my thatch of auburn hair.

My mum was pale and fair and always immaculately dressed. I don't think she ever saw me as a child. It was as if I was more like something to be dressed well and shown off to the neighbourhood. I went to tap lessons and ballet school and whenever there was a visitor I'd be made to perform. One year we went to a holiday camp and mum and dad entered me for the Prettiest Princess competition. I won and for the rest of the week I paraded about with a sash on. Of course I lapped it up. I was a precocious kid and everyone but my doting parents must have been heartily sick of me.

We never wanted for anything. Dad had a decent job as a fitter and we had a holiday every year. I had the best clothes from quality shops and I was always being rewarded for things that I did. When I passed my eleven-plus I was given a gorgeous pink bicycle with a white saddle. As I grew older, nobody was considered good enough for me to play with. Mum didn't like me going to other children's houses in case I caught something. In fact she didn't like me going further than the garden gate and I spent an increasing amount of my early childhood feeling rather lonely.

The only time I was allowed out on my own was when Uncle Ted paid a visit. He was an old friend of the family and a frequent visitor to our house but for some reason I took a dislike to him. Sometimes he called by in the day when dad was at work, and he'd let me take his terrier Rex for a walk up and down the back entry, the path which ran behind the length of our terrace. I remember coming back one day to find the door locked and the curtains drawn. I must have stored the information without giving it much thought and it only emerged several months later when mum and I were having a row. She was on at me about getting in a few minutes late from school and in an early fit of bitchiness I turned to her and said, "What about that day when Uncle Ted was here and the door was locked so I couldn't get in? Well I'm going to tell dad." I felt terrible for being so bold, but it must have hit home because mum went very quiet and turned away to get my tea ready.

After passing my eleven-plus I managed to disrupt Walley Range High School for Girls for about two years before being removed and sent to the secondary modern. School was an outlet for all the emotions I had to bottle up at home, where I was expected to behave as well as look like Lady Muck. Mum and dad had grown into the sort of people who thought that children should be seen and not heard, but maybe that was only to be expected having me around all the time. The older I got, the more I rebelled against their rules. I loved them very much, especially dad who thought the world of his little girl, but it didn't mean I wanted to sit around playing with dolls all day long. I desperately wanted to live with the glamorous family who moved in next door but one. Their life seemed free and easy and the parents went down to the pub twice a day on Saturdays leaving the kids to amuse themselves. My parents would have been shocked if they'd known, but as they had no idea what the new neighbours were like I was able to make friends without their disapproval. I'd learnt some cunning by this time and pretended to chum up with Margaret, who was thirteen like me but rather plain and studious, whereas it was really her older sister Alma – the outrageous one – I liked.

Margaret became my passport to freedom. While my parents thought I was playing round at her house, I was really out and about with Alma. We used to dress up together and wiggle our way up and down Stockport Road counting the wolf-whistles.

In those days – the mid-fifties – jiving was all the rage. A gang of us used to divide our time between a milk bar in Chapel Street, decked out in chrome, and a roller-skating rink with a juke box. By now mum and dad had realised the only way to hold me back was to lock me up. They knew they couldn't do that so they agreed to let me go out with certain approved friends. Of course I was always the one who had to be home early but I soon found ways round it.

On the night the gang went to see *Rock Around the Clock* in the Theatre Royal in Manchester, I told mum I was doing my homework at Margaret's house and then sneaked out with my clothes and make-up in a duffle bag. I changed into a skin-tight polo neck sweater and a flared skirt with layers of net underskirts. The cinema was packed out and we all started climbing up onto the seats and jiving to Bill Haley and the Comets. We were having a great time when suddenly a load of firemen arrived and turned their water hoses on us, and we had to travel the five miles back home soaked through with everybody on the bus staring at us. I was two and a half hours late getting in and the reception was cold enough to freeze the water still in my hair. Mum had developed a habit of switching off and totally ignoring me. It turned out to be one of the first symptoms of mental illness but I wasn't to know that and it hurt me terribly. I dreaded her moods much more than dad's temper, and this time the coldness in her eyes made me tremble. I was grounded for a fortnight and when I was allowed out again they kept a stricter eye on me than ever before. I had to promise to be back at a particular time and if I was more than half an hour late dad would call out the police. At first they took his calls seriously and I'd be fetched home by a copper in uniform, causing all the lace curtains in Gordon Avenue to twitch excitedly. But eventually the police got fed up with reports that I was missing and told dad to sit tight till his troublesome daughter came home.

I don't think I was particularly wild and I'd have much

preferred being open and honest with my parents. But by trying to keep me as a virtual prisoner and a showpiece rather than a lively young teenager, they forced me to tell fibs about my friends and what I was doing. If they'd only been prepared to bend a little in my direction, I think we'd have had a great relationship.

Boys and girls hung around together in our neighbourhood and Terry Henry was just one of the gang. He looked a bit like Tommy Steele, with blond curly hair sticking right out at the front in a Tony Curtis style and the tightest drainpipes you can imagine. I didn't fancy him especially, though we had strict parents in common and the fact that his widowed mother thought nothing was too good for him.

I adored his Teddy boy clothes and spent weeks plucking up the courage to ask mum for something fashionable. Eventually I persuaded her to order me a suit, and it wasn't till she saw me in it that she realised what she'd done. The colour was a respectable grey, but the skirt was so narrow I could hardly walk without falling over, and it had a fingertip jacket with a black velvet collar. If it hadn't cost so much I think she'd have cut it up as soon as she saw me come wobbling down the stairs in it.

We smoked in the milk bar of course, palming our cigarettes if any adult walked in, but it was all innocent fun. And gradually mum and dad gave me a bit more freedom, though never as much as the other kids. I tried bringing some of my friends home but mum was beginning to be very forgetful and I got embarrassed when she kept asking them the same questions over and over. I think some of them got frightened away. Colin certainly did, though by dad not mum. He was a real good-looker and he called for me one night to take me to Levenshulme Palais. I was about fourteen and as I was leaving I got the usual curfew warning from dad: "Sheila – don't forget. You are not to be back later than half past!" "Half past what?" Colin asked me, looking a bit put out. The Palais always had a live band and it didn't finish till midnight. "Half past eleven," I lied, knowing there'd be hell to pay if I wasn't back home an hour earlier, and I spent the rest of the evening worrying. It was bad enough having to drag Colin away from the band when it was still rocking and rolling, but my home-coming was even worse. We'd just stopped at the gate when the front door opened and dad started bawling at me, "What time do you think this is, young lady! This is the last time you're allowed out," and so it went on. I couldn't take the humiliation and Colin certainly wasn't the type to be sympathetic to girls who couldn't control their parents.

They were still imposing restrictions after I'd left school and got a job as an insurance clerk in the centre of Manchester. I may have been earning money, but I had to be in at half past six every evening. The girls in the office kept asking me to go dancing at the Plaza, where Jimmy Savile was manager. We often went there at lunchtime but for those who were really keen it was open in the evenings as well from five to seven thirty. Usually I'd make some excuse but one night I joined them. Of course I was late home and there was another row. Dad threatened to strop me for giving him a load of lip and mum said I was a little tart. "Just like your mother," she added, which made dad turn on her instead of me. That episode was the final straw. I'd had enough of being babied and I decided to run away. Later in the week I bundled some clothes in a case and went to some rather shady people I'd met who shared a house in Oppenshawe. It wasn't a very suitable place for a young girl but I was gradually being drawn to the attractions of life on the wrong side of the tracks. I might well have ended up in trouble if I'd stayed but in the three days it took for the police to fetch me all I'd done was dye my hair a horrible red.

The woman police sergeant who came for me was as hard as nails. She was angry too, because she'd been called out once too often by my father when I was late home. She advised my parents to teach me a lesson by refusing to have me back and I was sent for three weeks to a remand home called Burford House for being "beyond my parents' care and control". They were three of the longest weeks in my life, and mum and dad didn't come and see me once. I think they'd been told I'd be brought to heel quicker if they stayed away. After that I went to court and dad asked if I'd learned my lesson and planned to start behaving properly. "Not if it means coming home straight from work every night and only ever going out with you and mum on Friday nights to the cinema!" So that was that, and I got sent back to Burford House for another three weeks. It might have gone on like that forever but a woman welfare officer acted as a go-between, persuading my parents that they were being too strict, and me that I should learn to compromise. It did us a lot of good and we got back together on much better terms.

Because I was a good worker the insurance company were happy to have me back, but it wasn't for long. I woke up one day to find that my arm had locked in one position and I couldn't move it. It was during a polio scare and I was whisked into an isolation hospital. In fact I had rheumatic fever and I was allowed out after a few weeks, but during that time I had a very sweet letter from Terry Henry asking me to go out with him.

Before this our relationship had consisted of holding hands and having the odd kiss in a doorway. But now most of our friends were paired off and one of the boys told Terry that he and his girl had gone the whole way. Early one evening, a few months before my sixteenth birthday, we thought we'd do the same in a shed in the local park. I was wearing a white skirt and when it was over, which seemed quite soon, I stood up and we noticed there was blood all over it. We really panicked then. Terry tried wiping it off with water from the park tap which only made it ten times worse. When I got home I tried backing in through the hallway and upstairs before mum could notice. But it was useless trying to hide something like that from someone who watched my every mood and kept account of every period. "I know what you've been up to," she said the moment I got in. I was scared silly and hissed at her: "If you accuse me one more time, I'm off! And don't go telling my dad what's on your dirty mind."

I can't say I gave the episode much thought till I missed my next period. It was just as well mum was in one of her funny moods or she'd have realised something was wrong, but her mind seemed elsewhere. I took the sanitary towels she left for me in the bathroom and got rid of them one by one. "You can't be pregnant," was Terry's response when I told him.

"We only did it once and I don't think we did it properly." We tried doing it properly a fortnight later, thinking a second go might start me bleeding. It was Sunday and Terry's mum had gone to mass. We were at it in the front room when his elder brother Liam walked in. He just apologised and walked straight out again, but I think it was then I realised that nothing Terry and I did would ever work out right.

When I was about three months gone my dad looked at me hard one night at tea and said, "Sheila, you're like a sack of potatoes round the middle. Haven't you got something to tell me?" I felt awful. I'd let him down, abused his trust, and I had nothing to say. I didn't have any idea about what was going to happen to me but by the end of the week it was all horribly clear. Mrs Henry had been consulted, the priest had been informed and the church booked. I'd even had the first fitting for a wedding dress.

It was a white dress with a drop waist and I wore it with winkle-pickers. On the day of the wedding – 30th July 1957 – my father told me, "You don't have to go through with this, you know, if you don't want to," but it was a bit bloody late by then. If he'd said it three or four weeks earlier I wouldn't have married and Terry and me would have been a lot happier.

My seventeen-year-old husband worked in the tripe factory and we went to live in his mother's house in Longsight. She charged us five pounds a week and every time I wanted a bath I had to pay for it. She cooked the evening meal and whenever Terry got a chop, I was given a sausage instead. He used to cut me mouthfuls of his food and pass them over when she wasn't looking but he never dared complain to her face. I busied myself during the day with chores. I'd wash Terry's shirts and put them out on the line, and then Mrs Henry would bring them all in again saying I hadn't done them properly. When I ironed his shirts and folded them up, she unfolded them and did them again. After six months of her carping I couldn't take any more and Terry and me moved into mum and dad's house in Gordon Avenue.

It was there that I went into labour. And I stayed in labour for over ten hours till the baby showed signs of distress and had to be dragged out by forceps. She was christened Donna and lived for seventeen hours. When it was all over I remember thinking that I'd landed myself with a husband I didn't really want and a mother-in-law I disliked and that it was all for nothing.

Chapter 2

THIRD TIME LUCKY

By the time I was twenty and Terry was twenty-one, I'd already lost two babies. The next baby after Donna was stillborn. Then I fell for the third time. We'd just moved into our own home in Ratcliffe Street and had been busy doing it up. One of the first things we did was to paint the front blue and white in support of Manchester City. We thought the landlord would throw us out when he saw what we'd done, but he was so chuffed he gave us a week rent-free. Terry was at the tripe works, boiling and purifying till his hair and clothes stank and I was fulfilling an ambition I'd had since I was a child – to train as a nurse at the Manchester Royal Infirmary. I was completely absorbed in my nursing, so much so that I didn't really want to take my days off. Besides, going out with Terry wasn't much fun because he was absurdly jealous. He didn't even want me to sit on the long seat of the bus when we went into town because it meant other people could look at my legs! We had a limited social life. In those days you always went out together as a married couple and the only friends you had were other couples. Apart from a Saturday night visit to the pub, the highlight of my week was Friday's trip to the wash-house. Imagine anyone looking forward to going to a wash-house, but I did! It was a chance to get out on my own and meet other people. One of us would take a flask, another some butties, and we'd sit there having a good old chinwag.

I knew I was pregnant the moment I started being sick. It was only four or five days after I conceived but by now I knew the terrible symptoms. I went straight off to my GP, Dr Lesley Joseph. He'd known me since I was a child and I trusted him like a friend. "I might be able to help you this time, Sheila," he said. "I've got something here which I'd like you to try for me." I can still see him now, a bit untidy and very overweight. He walked over to a glass-fronted cabinet and took out this bottle of small white tablets. "Try these," he said, "and let me know what you think of them."

At first I took one every morning and I thought they were marvellous. The name on the bottle was Distaval and Dr Joseph said they'd proved very successful in curing morning sickness. He said I could take two or three if I needed them and I found that if I took one before I went to bed, it stopped me feeling sick till about lunchtime. Then Dr Joseph gave me a prescription and I carried on taking them till I was about three months pregnant.

During that time I felt really well, much better than in my first two pregnancies. The only drawback was having to give up my nursing a few months before the final exams which would have made me a State Enrolled Nurse, but it was a sacrifice I was prepared to make for a healthy baby. Terry and I were getting along pretty well, although he was always acting the kid and never taking any responsibility. At twenty my life had settled into a very even, contented pattern, with the house to fuss over and mum and dad living round the corner. I got it into my head that as long as I didn't move about too much, this pregnancy would be fine and I really pampered myself, put my feet up a lot, and refused to carry more than a few bits of shopping at a time. When we went to a fairground one day I refused to go on any of the rides in case the slightest bump started off a miscarriage. My friends thought I was becoming a wet blanket and Terry hadn't realised that having a baby would be such hard work.

It was about this time that Doreen Walker asked me to go with her to a spiritualist at some old house on Stockport Road in Levenshulme. I thought spiritualism was a load of rubbish but as Doreen couldn't find anyone else daft enough to go along, I went with her to keep her company. There were about fifteen of us sitting on rows of chairs in a big front room while a grey-haired old woman stood at the front giving out messages from the other side about what Uncle George had said or how dear Edith was still at peace. I was right at the back waiting for her to come up with something for Doreen but all of a sudden she pointed at me.

"You're pregnant," she said, "but I'm very sorry, my love, there's something terribly wrong with this child. You're going to have a lot of heartache." Then she said she was getting another feeling that I would really love the baby and, with that, she passed on to someone else. I sat feeling completely blank until it was all over and we went outside. Doreen looked at me and said, "What's the matter with your baby then?" I said, "Don't be so stupid, you can't believe that bloody nonsense." I was that sort of person, very matter-of-fact. Doreen wondered how the woman had known I was pregnant, because I wasn't very big, but I guessed someone in the audience may have known me and told her.

Anyway, I didn't give it a second thought, not even weeks later when I did start to sense that there was something wrong. After four and a half months the baby still hadn't started moving. When I told them at St Mary's antenatal clinic, they sent me off for an X-ray. There wasn't such a thing as ultrasound in those days, so this was the only way of looking at the foetus if you suspected something was wrong. I was told to report to my own doctor a week later. That Friday morning Dr Joseph was in a terrible state. He flapped about, asked after my mother, sat down, stood up, went to his medicine cabinet, then back to his desk, sat down again and looked hard at some papers on his desk. Finally, he managed to say that my X-ray showed that the child I was carrying had got no arms and there was some deformity in the lower limbs though he wasn't sure what. He then suggested I have the baby at home. He thought there was little hope of the baby living, and I think he was trying to spare me the agony of seeing other mums with their babies. He seemed to have tears in his eyes. After all that he offered me a drink! But I didn't want his whisky or his helplessness. I don't remember anything after that, not even going home.

After losing my first two babies I'd come to the conclusion that I couldn't do anything right, not even the thing that was supposed to come most naturally to a woman. Now I wondered if this was God's punishment for all the times I'd sneaked off to enjoy myself behind my parents' backs.

Everything the doctors said added to the impression that it was somehow my fault. At St Mary's Hospital they started questioning me about what pills I'd taken and whether my GP had given me any other tablets apart from Distaval. They seemed suspicious and cross with me, and it was easy to forget that I was the one who had a right to get upset. What made it all worse was that no-one except dad would believe me when I told them what was wrong with the baby.

Terry said the X-ray pictures were rubbish and the doctors didn't know what they were talking about. He even got his sister-in-law who was a nurse to examine me and she said there was so much fluid that they couldn't possibly have seen the baby clearly. She just said that to the family because it was what they wanted to hear. There was no point even talking to my mother because by now her mental condition had deteriorated. She was slipping into premature senility and half the time she didn't understand what was going on around her. The only person I could talk to, apart from dad, was an old school-friend called Iris. She and her mum, Mrs Hampson, lived at the back of our road and they were really good neighbours. As it happened, Iris had just had a baby girl and she said that, if the doctors were wrong and my baby lived, I could have all her clothes and equipment.

Terry's family refused to accept what the doctors said even after they'd taken a second X-ray. That was a terrible experience because in those days they held you down on a hard bed with two straps, which they'd tighten with a lever till your stomach was as flat as it could be. The woman doing the X-ray, though, was wonderful. She showed me all the pictures and explained everything to me, and it was then that she told me I was carrying a girl. She was the only person who talked about her as if she was a human being. The rest of the doctors didn't like talking about her at all. They told me not to prepare for the baby. It was a case of hanging on for the next four or five months, they said, getting the delivery over and done with and then just carrying on with life as if nothing had ever happened.

The only time I thought they might be wrong about her dying was at about seven months when she started to move.

There wasn't much of her obviously, but it was a lovely feeling. She was lying underneath my ribcage and at nine o'clock every evening it felt as if she was putting her head out, waggling it about for five minutes and then sticking it back in on the other side. It was then that I started to get these mixed feelings. I began to wonder whether they were right in saying she wouldn't live.

I think that most of this time I was in a complete daze. It was as if part of my brain had gone dead. But I do remember wishing that the staff at St Mary's wouldn't behave as if my pregnancy was something unpleasant that I'd brought in. They didn't seem interested in me at all. They didn't seem to bother about whether I was anaemic or anything. In fact, one month I felt so tired that I stood and demanded a blood test. All I wanted was to be treated like all the other mums. Ridiculous as it sounds, I just wanted to lie on the bed and have my tummy prodded. Sometimes I wondered why I bothered to go to the antenatal clinic because nobody really bothered with me.

I should have had the baby in March, but at the end of the month they were still debating what to do. Then we got into April and on about the twentieth somebody decided something had to be done to get her out of me. They took me into the new maternity wing at St Mary's, broke my waters late on Sunday evening, and I went into labour on Monday, 23rd April. On Tuesday afternoon, three or four hours before she was born, one of her little feet appeared. Then the doctors started arriving in the delivery room. Obviously they were all coming in to see what I'd given birth to. I should have told them all to go to hell, but you don't know how to stand up for yourself when you're only twenty and you can't see the door for doctors. They had my legs up in stirrups and I felt as though I was on show. One after another they came in, looked at the little foot flapping about, and then went away again without saying anything.

She was born at ten past six and suddenly it was panic stations. They had to suck her out and afterwards they told me she was nearly black from being so overdue. Although I'd been told it was a girl, I wanted to be sure so I asked what it was I'd had but no-one would tell me. They just kept passing it down the line – "Sister will tell you", "The doctor will talk to you in a moment".

It was then that I lost my temper. "I'm only bloody well asking you what I've had. I know it's got no arms!" That stopped them in their tracks. "If you don't tell me what I've had," I went on, "I'll jump off this table and go and look for myself." It was a stupid thing to say with my arms fastened to drips and my legs stuck up in the air, but it made me feel better. Until now I'd passively suffered all the indignities, the medical discussions held over my head, never to my face, and the constant interrogation as if I were to blame, and I'd never once shown any anger. But deep inside there was a sense of rage that fate, or God, could be so cruel as to make my baby deformed. Anyway my outburst seemed to worry them and they sent for the senior consultant. It was ages before he arrived and I was feeling really sore. I needed thirty-two stitches but they didn't get round to doing them till seven o'clock, when I begged the nurse to take my legs out of the stirrups. When at last the consultant came he told me that my baby was a girl. I asked about her legs and he said she hadn't really got any, all she had were thighs and little feet, and no arms at all. He then surprised me by asking what I was going to call her. I thought it was because she was about to be baptised and told him I'd like to call her Janette. "Is she going to die, then?" I asked. "Not at this particular moment," he said, giving me such a peculiar look. "She's deafening us with her crying."

I didn't want to see Janette straightaway, but I was told that Terry was in with her. Soon he came along to see me. His face was grey and he said, "It was horrible. I thought I was going to throw up." But he didn't really seem to have any emotions about his baby and he never asked me how I felt. Not that he'd have got much of a reply. At that time I seemed to have cut myself off from all feelings. It was as if I were dead inside. Terry started talking about what I wanted to do with "it" and something in the tone of his voice momentarily sparked off the anger again. I said I'd give it some thought but that she wasn't an it, she was a little girl. His reaction put a huge gulf between us. It was as if the baby had nothing to do with him. I was entirely to blame for messing things up yet again, and I'd have to get us out of the mess. If he'd shown any signs of being sorry for me or himself or the baby I dare say I'd have broken down and we could have cried together. But he didn't and I asked him to leave me alone so I could sleep.

On the ward the next morning a few women came and asked me what I'd had and I just said my baby was a girl. All the babies were brought in except for her, and when a nurse said she'd bring a wheelchair and take me out to see her, I said no thank you. A few hours later the paediatrician did his round of the ward, starting at the bed opposite mine and working his way slowly round looking at all the babies. At last it was my turn. He stood by the bed and said, "Well, Mrs Henry, I suppose you know what's wrong with your baby?"

He told me there was a chance she had water on the brain but they couldn't be certain and then he said, "Now, from what I can gather from your husband and your family, you won't be taking this baby home." I told him that was my decision, not his, and when he said how foolish it would be for me to keep her, I asked him what he intended to do with her if I left her in the hospital. "There are places where we can send these babies," he said, and he got me to promise that I'd think about it before he came again later that afternoon.

I found out from Terry at visiting time that the place they had in mind for Janette was in London. He said they'd be bringing me a consent form to sign. As he walked in, I half expected him to be carrying a bunch of flowers like all the other fathers but he was empty-handed. All the time I was in the hospital I only received one bouquet, which was from my dad, and no cards. I don't think Terry told our friends and neighbours that I'd had the baby, though they must have been wondering where I was and what was going on. His mum didn't come to see me either, even though she worked in the hospital kitchens. But when my parents arrived, dad put his arms round me and called me "Love" and asked me how I was. As his only child, he'd always done everything he could for me. He said we'd go away on holiday when I was better. My mother just sat there nodding, not understanding what was

going on or being said. Dad never mentioned the baby because they'd told him I didn't want anything to do with her
and was going to send her away.

After that, people kept coming and going, expecting me to
make my decision. A middle-aged woman came with the
consent form but I sent her away. The doctor came again that
evening but I still wouldn't agree to their plan. I knew they
were waiting for me to break down, to show some emotion,
but I wouldn't give them that satisfaction. I wouldn't cry.
They even sent a psychiatrist to see me and he asked what I
was feeling inside, and what I felt about my daughter. "I don't
feel anything," I replied. "How can I when I haven't seen her
yet?" "But do you think you'd want to harm her . . . ?" and so
it went on with him writing all my answers down.

By now I was the only person in the ward who hadn't seen
my daughter. She was in the nursery with the other babies so
all the other mothers had had a good look. Not that they said
anything about her to me. If they did come up and talk to me
it was about anything under the sun except that. They'd ask
me where I lived and what I did for work and then they'd get
back to their beds, relieved to have got the chat over and
done with. I sat looking out of the window at a cloudless blue
sky, my feelings completely numb. It was when I remembered
that the woman would soon be coming back with her consent
forms that I suddenly realised what I was going to do. I'd tell
her to stuff her forms. It was twenty to twelve, three days after
I'd had Janette, and the nurses were just wheeling in the
dinner trolley and beginning to serve out plates of lamb and
mashed potato.

"Can I see my baby now, please," I demanded loudly. The
nurse at my bedside looked startled and asked if I'd wait till all
the patients had eaten their dinner. Perhaps she didn't want
to put them off their food. I said no, I couldn't wait, I wanted
to see her now. What's more, I wanted them to bring her
without any clothes on, just with a cover over her. That
Easter of 1962 was unusually hot and she didn't need to be
wrapped up. The nurse looked at me and I could see that she
thought I was about to flip my lid, but she put down her
serving ladle and slowly walked off to the nursery.

When I saw her walk back into the ward with a bundle in her arms, I asked her to draw the screens round my bed and leave us together. I wanted us to be alone, just me and my baby. I took hold of the bundle. It took me about five minutes before I could draw the covers back. It was the hardest thing I'd ever had to do in my life till then. The baby opened her eyes and I thought, "Poor little sod, as well as everything else wrong with you, you're cross-eyed!" But it was at that moment that I knew how tightly we were bound together, Janette and me. I just held her, that little body with no arms and with two little feet like flippers, and she nestled her head into the nape of my neck. I'll never forget that moment. "You're not going anywhere," I said. "The only place you're going is home with me." That's when my real fight started.

After that I began feeding Janette in the nursery like the other mums. There was another baby girl in there at the time, who ended up going to the same school as Janette. She was called Susan and she had all her limbs, and a beautiful face, but she was brain-damaged. I remember looking at Susan and then looking at Janette lying beside her, and wondering why the God up there couldn't just have made one perfect child for at least one of us. I said as much to Susan's mum and she started crying, but to me it was just common sense.

When Terry next came I was feeding Janette in the nursery. He was surprised to see me there and the first thing he asked was about the consent form. When I told him I was keeping the baby he was stupefied. For ages he stood there looking at me in horror, not saying anything. Then he said, "What will people say?" and I told him I didn't give a shitty nappy what people said, I was bringing her home. Terry was shaking but he managed to say, "I'm telling you now, if you bring that home, I'm leaving."

"Well go home then and pack your bags," was my reply. "And tell dad I want to see him." I felt as bold as brass, I knew exactly what I wanted, and I wasn't going to waste any more time being messed about by doctors, nurses or husbands!

Dad got time off work to come and see me and when I told him that I was going to bring her home he said, "Why not? She's your baby." He promised to go and see Mrs Hampson and ask if we could take up her offer of baby clothes. Because they'd told me the baby wouldn't live, I didn't have a single thing for Janette. Dad took a long list away with him and left me to wait for the doctor.

I remember thinking, as the doctor strolled in, what a nasty face he had, but I suppose that was because what he wanted me to do seemed so horrible. He was arrogant and bullying, as if only he knew what was right for my baby and I was too stupid to make any decision. He said I couldn't possibly know what I was doing. The child probably wouldn't live, and if she did she'd never be able to talk and she wouldn't be able to sit up, and so the arguments went on. But I told him I didn't care what he thought, and it was a chance I had to take. "If she is going to die, at least I can give her some love before she goes." He gave up on me then and turned away with a sigh. I could see the nurses clustering round him at the entrance to the ward, talking in pained tones about my unbalanced behaviour.

From that moment the hospital staff completely lost interest in me and Janette. I wanted to leave Janette in the hospital while I went home to get things ready and I asked the sister if I could come back at feeding times until I had everything I needed. That was the start of another lecture about what a foolish girl I was and how I'd be saddling myself for life with an invalid. There was no question of giving me any advice about how to cope with a handicapped child and my request was flatly refused. In the end, I had to stay in St Mary's for seventeen days because I'd got an infection in my stitches, and it was only Janette, dad's visits, and messages from Iris and Mrs Hampson that kept me going.

During my last few days on the ward, dad brought me some bad news. Dr Joseph had died of a heart attack. It was a big shock because he was only forty, though he was overweight. Dad had been told that he regained consciousness once before he died and his first words were, "Has Sheila Henry had that baby yet?" In those days there was no publicity about the danger of thalidomide, and of course he gave me those pills in good faith, but obviously what happened to Janette had been preying on his mind.

Chapter 3

BRINGING MY BABY BACK HOME

On the day I brought Janette home there was a fresh wind blowing and I kept her well wrapped up. I couldn't go to the house in Ratcliffe Street because Terry was living there. His decision to have nothing to do with the baby remained as firm as ever but I knew my future lay with my daughter and I hardly cared whether he'd be part of it or not. It was my dad who was sticking by me and Janette and it was dad who made a home for us in Gordon Avenue. As I walked through the door the first thing I noticed were the nappies. They'd been washed and were drying over the fireguard, hanging from the furniture, draped everywhere. Dad had made up a bed for me in the front room and lit a fire. It looked really welcoming and I wanted to hug him but when I looked round, he'd disappeared. He still hadn't seen Janette and didn't show any sign of wanting to look at her. I think he was waiting to face her in his own time.

Normally whenever anybody in our street came home with a baby, all the neighbours would be round in moments to have a good peek. But there wasn't a soul on the doorstep except for dear little Mrs Hampson, dressed as always in her pinny. As soon as I saw her, plump and smiling, I guessed who'd been helping dad with all those nappies. She bustled into my new room, where Janette was already installed in her cot. I warned her, "You do know she hasn't got any arms, don't you?" "Has she got a face?" was her reply. "Has she got any lips? Well that'll do me then. All I want to do is give her a big kiss!" Her saying that meant more to me than anything and it helped enormously in the months to come.

We left Janette asleep in her crib and joined dad in the kitchen. After we'd had a cup of tea, he suddenly announced that he was going into the front room. After about an hour he came out with Janette in his arms and I could see he'd been crying. He handed her to my mum, who just kept kissing her till I thought she'd smother her. Poor mum was so far gone by now that I don't think she realised there was anything wrong with her first grandchild. Anyway, after that moment everything in dad's world was for Janette. He worshipped her and everything she wanted he'd try to give her. There was definitely something special between the two of them, and I suppose it was because he partly took on the role of a father.

Terry was still determined not to see or acknowledge his child but I had to go and see him every Thursday evening to pick up my maintenance and sometimes I took Janette with me. Terry never once picked her up or made any comment about her, but I insisted on telling him exactly what she'd been doing, whether she'd slept or had wind, or smiled. I could see it irritated him and that made me feel sad. I can't say I loved him and perhaps I never had, but I still had dreams about us being a proper married couple who could coo and gurgle over their first-born child. Strangely, though, I never blamed Terry for pushing us out. Like him, I saw Janette as my baby and my responsibility. Even though I didn't know for certain that the pills were to blame for the way she was, I assumed it was my fault and not his. I was the guilty one. But the one thing that really steamed me up was the way he and his family seemed to ignore Janette as if, by pretending she wasn't there, she'd disappear and everything would be normal again. I still felt bitter that his mother hadn't even visited us in the hospital where she worked. So after four weeks I decided to confront her.

I dressed Janette in her best clothes, wrapped her in a blanket and took her over to Terry's mum's. Mrs Henry peered at her for a brief, half-hearted moment, muttered something but made no attempt to hold Janette. I could hardly believe it but I stayed anyway for a cup of tea with her. When I said I had to go she walked with me towards the bus-stop and one of her neighbours rushed up to us and said, "Oh do let me see the baby. Can I hold her?" Before I had a chance to reply Mrs Henry jumped in with an excuse about Janette being asleep and tugged me away by the sleeve. It turned out she'd kept the whole thing a big secret.

I was determined that she should recognise her grand-daughter and forced myself to make another visit. It was a gorgeously hot day and I left Janette in the front garden, by the bay window. She was lying in the big black and white pram dad had bought for her, under the canopy, with the covers drawn back. She had a pretty dress on and I suppose that by now I'd almost forgotten that she looked different from other babies. But Terry's mother hadn't forgotten. I was busy in the kitchen peeling potatoes for the dinner, going out every few minutes to check my baby was all right, like any other mum. Every time I checked, I found the covers had been pulled over her so I drew them back again. It happened about four or five times and each time Janette looked hotter and more uncomfortable. She was red in the face and sweating. The next time Mrs Henry came into the kitchen I shouted at her not to dare to cover up my baby. She gave me a withering look and told me she wasn't having her neighbours seeing she'd got "that thing" as a granddaughter. I was so angry I lashed out at her with the knife still in my hand and cut her on the arm. I don't think it was on purpose though I can't be sure. She started to scream and rushed next door to fetch Terry's sister. After that she went round telling everyone that I was a raving lunatic – and at the time she was probably right.

I couldn't blame people for their attitude towards Janette. No-one had ever come across such deformities in a baby before then and people are always scared by anything differ-ent. Janette was certainly that, in all sorts of ways, and it wasn't until the news stories and other publicity about the plight of the thalidomide children started appearing that people started becoming more sympathetic in their behaviour. Once they got to know Janette, then of course they started to respond to her as an individual human being, not as a side-show freak. For some people, though, she was never anything but an embarrassment. None of my in-laws, for example, wanted anything to do with Janette, except Terry's sister-in-law Joyce. She was the only one who had bought a present for the baby – a yellow pram-set in a box. As far as the others were concerned, she might never have been born. And several of my friends just seemed to vanish. There was a girl called Ethel who'd been carrying her baby at the same time as I was carrying Janette. She'd given birth a week before me and she lived round the corner from Gordon Avenue. Soon after I came home I saw her walking down the street in my direction. We were obviously both heading for the same shortcut to the shops so I called out to her and she froze in her tracks. Then she wheeled her pram round, shouted something about having forgotten the baby's bottle and hurried back up the road. Fortunately I still had Iris, and eventually Doreen braced herself for a visit so I wasn't entirely deserted. But I missed out on chats with other young mums, swopping notes about night feeds and teething. And I got used to either being ignored or stared at by strangers. I soon made up my mind that I wasn't going to stop taking my baby out in her lovely pram just because it seemed to upset so many people. And the fact that she wasn't a conventionally pretty baby with chubby arms and legs didn't mean I couldn't dress her up in bows and frills. Once I put her in a new cotton frock with smocking at the front, and left her outside a shop while I bought some cigarettes. But when I came out and looked in the pram I nearly died of shock because the dress was back to front. I thought, "God, her head's swivelled round!" not realising that she'd been shuffling about in her pram and it was her dress that had shifted, not her head. That was the first of many times that Janette's agility caught me on the hop.

I was shopping over in Longsight one morning and I came out of a supermarket to find a woman standing by the pram. "Oh no, not another comment!" I thought, bracing myself for some hurtful remark. But she smiled at me and said, "I know your mum." Well of course I thought she meant my adoptive mum and I muttered something about her not being very well. "No, I don't mean that mum," she said. "I mean your real mum, Ann." I suppose I should have said that I only knew one mum and dad and left it at that, but curiosity got the better of me and I asked where this real mother was. She had the address and gave it to me on a scrap of paper. It was as if she'd come with a message that my mother wanted to see me but, foolishly, I never asked her how she knew about me or who she was, or whether this mother of mine really wanted to see me. I kept the scrap of paper in my purse for the next fortnight, not saying a word to anyone about it. But one day as soon as I woke up I knew it was the day I was going to look for my mother.

The address was in Hulme which was quite a distance away, but I got on a bus with Janette and off we went. It was a very working-class area, with rows and rows of terraced houses with doors leading straight off the street. I walked up and down for about an hour until I found the right house. It had a red door, and there were some grubby, half-caste children playing outside who all stared at me, making me feel very embarrassed. A boy answered the door and I asked if Ann was in and to tell her that Sheila was here, as if she'd know immediately who Sheila was. A few moments later this woman sauntered up to the door. She was little, like me, but that was the only thing we had in common. She was blonde and a bit worn at the edges.

"Hello, you'd better come in," she said as casually as if she'd never been in my life or out of it. "I'm busy," she said over her shoulder as I followed her in, feeling a mixture of confusion and disappointment. I don't know what I'd expected, but it wasn't this. There was a black man in the hall dressed in a boiler suit and carrying a step-ladder. I was thinking it must be a painter who'd come to decorate the house, which certainly needed a bit of attention, but she introduced him as her husband. It was the first time I'd met a mixed-race couple and I felt shocked and disgusted. Shameful though it is to recall it, that was everyone's response then to white girls marrying or living with black men. It was even worse when I realised that the coloured children I'd seen outside were my half-brothers and sisters. The next blow was when I was introduced to a girl who can only have been about eighteen months younger than me, so my mother hadn't been long in making the same mistake twice.

In all this time, the woman who presumably at some time had briefly held me in her arms, didn't once look at the baby in my arms or show any interest in me whatsoever. She just offered me a cup of tea as if I was a neighbour who'd dropped round to scrounge some sugar. If I'd been hoping for some display of emotion, some warm-hearted tearful reunion, I'd have to forget it quickly. In fact all I felt now was a bad sensation at the pit of my stomach as if I'd eaten something that disagreed with me. If I hadn't been holding Janette I think I'd have run out of the house there and then and off down the street, but I managed to stay where I was for a few minutes more. Then I made some excuse about having to get back and left, with Ann showing no more enthusiasm for my going than she had for my coming. It was very puzzling and hurtful and as I was walking back I was pleading with God for me to make a better job of motherhood myself.

Later, when I was living with a black man myself and had half-caste children of my own, I went back to Hulme to see if I could try to establish some sort of relationship with my mother, with better grace and better understanding. But I found the rows of terraced houses had been pulled down and the man in a grocer's shop said the residents had been rehoused in Wythenshawe. I could have pursued it, but somehow felt it was better to leave things be.

My adoptive mum was in a crazy world of her own but dad made me as comfortable as he could at Gordon Avenue, and he was always glad to look after Janette. I can't pretend life wasn't a bit boring without a husband or boyfriend to take me out. Although I was tired because Janette was such a fretful baby who never slept for very long, I used to get so restless that I looked forward to my Thursday meetings with Terry, especially when it included going to the pub. We'd been apart for about five months when, after a few pints of beer and a Martini, we decided we'd have another go at living together. He moved in with me in Gordon Avenue and we struggled through a week but I couldn't accept his attitude towards Janette. He wouldn't do anything for her, not even pick her up if she was crying, and yet he resented it when I paid her any attention. I think he was jealous of dad too, because he knew that dad was the only one who really gave us any support. We had some fun that week but we had to agree that it wouldn't work and so Terry pushed off. Ten days later I woke up feeling sick – I'd conceived again.

My marriage was finished, I had one very demanding disabled baby to look after, and now I was pregnant again. Yet there was one part of me that really wanted another baby. Although doctors at the baby clinic had murmured about the drug Distaval and suggested that this could have damaged Janette, I still wasn't sure. After all, I'd lost two babies before having her and I hadn't taken any pills then. I wanted to prove that I could have an ordinary child with no deformities whatsoever and this fourth pregnancy gave me another chance. That was more important to me than the fact I'd be bringing up another baby without a father. My own dad couldn't understand this at all. He thought I shouldn't have any more children but devote my whole life to Janette. He even put money on the table for an abortion, something I'd never dreamt he'd do. "How do you know you're not going to go through the same thing all over again?" he said, but I'd no more listen to his kindly advice than support Manchester United.

It was the beginning of another battle. I was sick for twelve weeks and completely knackered because Janette still wasn't sleeping through the night, but of course this time I wouldn't take medicine of any sort, not even an iron tablet. As well as attending the antenatal clinic, I had to trudge back and forth each week to the baby clinic at St Mary's so that Janette could be used as a guinea-pig for all the doctors. I didn't know it, but the medical journals were now full of the word thalidomide, the actual drug sold in Britain as Distaval, and every time we went there were new doctors eager to explore where medical science had gone wrong. They came from all over the world and by the end of our visits there wasn't a part of Janette that hadn't been prodded, measured and analysed. She was a bad-tempered little thing and she objected to this weekly ritual. I'd just about had enough of it myself when one day they proudly said, "There's a consultant from London coming next week specially to examine Janette, so we'll see you then." I told them they could stuff their consultants and added, "You can find some other baby to experiment on because you're not having mine!" I stopped going after that.

When I was four and a half months pregnant I was called for an X-ray and told that if there was any sign of abnormality they'd abort the foetus. I remembered the discomfort from my last pregnancy – having to lie in a cold room with my tummy flattened with straps – but this time it was worth it. I had the same woman radiographer and she was almost as delighted as I was when she saw that the foetus was fine and it was a boy. I rushed back in the afternoon to tell Mrs Hampson and we had a glass of sherry to celebrate.

At the antenatal clinic they started on at me to send Janette away, saying that I surely couldn't manage with her and a new baby. I think the word had got round that I was a stroppy bitch who wouldn't take Janette to the kind doctors at the baby clinic and they didn't believe that I could manage without their help. I had to promise to let the hospital social workers know if I had the slightest problem, as if I'd agree to send my Janette away when the baby was born. I knew she'd be jealous enough without that.

How right I was! Neil was born on 24th July 1963 – a strapping ten-pounder and absolutely perfect. I thought he was beautiful but Janette couldn't stand the sight of him. There we were in the front room at dad's house, Neil in his crib and Janette screwing up her face and yelling blue murder if I so much as looked at him. I thought it was safe to leave them together because, although sixteen months old, she wasn't mobile. But one day when Neil was about three weeks old I left them in the sitting-room while I went to make a cup of tea. Suddenly there was an almighty squealing noise and I rushed back to find that Janette had shuffled on her bottom to the settee where I'd left Neil, and bitten him.

The experts had told me not to expect Janette to talk or show much intelligence, but she soon proved them wrong. She was talking by the time she was one year old, and her first words were: "Dink o' water". Dad and I just looked at each other in astonishment; then at the budgie. Mind you, that was pretty daft because we'd had the budgie for four years and it had never said a word. Anyway, it wasn't long before she was talking in proper sentences. Whenever Neil cried, she'd knit her brows and say to me, "If you pick that baby up I'll scream!" and she would. Her screech reminded Mrs Hampson of the old air-raid sirens. Consequently I hardly dared cuddle poor Neil, who spent a lot of time lying on a cushion with a bottle in his mouth while I sat several feet away watching them both.

Janette gave up her daytime sleep as soon as Neil was born. She was full of pent-up energy and soon learned how to follow me round with remarkable speed by sitting on her potty and wobbling from side to side. She had a very straight back and enough strength to steer herself, though the little flippers that were her feet didn't even touch the ground. Those feet were very tender, and because they bent backwards they made rolling difficult. But if Janette wanted to move without the aid of her potty, she'd look round for a piece of furniture that was low enough for her to lean on with her chin. She'd work her way towards it, and lever herself up into a sitting position, or she'd use her back to wriggle upright. She was very affection-ate and liked to sit between my legs when I was in an easy chair. I never rearranged the room to suit her or treated her in a special way. Meal-times were no problem either. She sat on the table with a tray at the right height in front of her, and ate with her mouth. She could make sandwiches by holding a baby's fork in her mouth, using it to pick up pieces of food and put them on her bread, then fold the bread over with her chin. A real redhead was Janette, with the temper of a sergeant-major and enough determination for an army.

Many thalidomide children had things wrong with their internal organs but Janette was lucky. It was only the parts of her you could see that were damaged, like her teeth. When they came through they were chipped and yellow, with no enamel on them. I still found coping with people's reactions to her difficult. Most people in Levenshulme had got used to seeing this toddler without arms or legs but once in the park I found two old ladies muttering to one another over her head. One of them was saying, "If I had something like that, I wouldn't bring it out of doors, would you?" so I told them to get knotted. I was learning to hide my hurt feelings under a hard shell, and I took to fighting back with insults of my own.

Eventually I grew tough enough to put up with all the un-kindness without even flinching. I wasn't ashamed of Janette and I was determined to take her out with me as much as possible, whatever people thought.

When she was eight months old she was given a pair of cosmetic arms which were just like doll's arms, made out of plastic. I was carrying her onto a bus one day when one of the arms got stuck. As I was giving a good tug, a woman behind me started screaming, "The baby's arm's got caught! Watch out or you'll break her arm off!" and she grabbed hold of Janette's hand. When she felt the hard plastic she recoiled in horror and, as the bus pulled away she was left on the pave-ment gawping. Janette had a wonderful sense of humour even at that age and she couldn't stop giggling but that poor woman must have had the shock of her life. I stopped putting the arms on after that, except for photographs.

Looking after Janette was a matter of trial and error. I didn't know anyone else with a disabled child, and I wasn't assigned a social worker so there was no-one to tell me what I should be doing. The only time I got any professional advice was when I took Janette to the hospital for a check-up. When she was sixteen months old, an age when other children are walking, the doctors said she should have artificial legs and I took her to Withington hospital for a fitting. They weren't legs as such, more like a pair of buckets with rockers at the bottom. I had to force her feet into leather tubes and then strap her into these bucket contraptions. I don't know whether it was worse for her or me. I had to bend her little feet forwards to fit the tubes and she'd yelp with pain every time they were touched, making me feel like a torturer. I had to bribe her with any-thing I could think of. She loved painting and I told her that if she wore the rockers she could stand at a proper easel, but it only worked once. And then she produced a diabolic trick which was to wait till I'd got her strapped in before announc-ing that she needed the potty. That meant that the whole thing had to be undone and I didn't have the energy to start again. She never felt secure on those rockers and looking back on it, I think it was a complete waste of time.

What Janette was lacking in limbs, she made up for in

brains. She never stopped talking and asking questions. But with all this I was becoming a nervous wreck. Ever since Janette had been born I'd had a tremor in my head which was particularly severe when I was tired, which was most of the time. It had started about a week after the birth. I'd woken up one night in a cold sweat, to find that I couldn't move my arms or legs and when I tried to call out for help no words came. The panic probably only lasted a few seconds but it seemed like ages and when I told Mrs Hampson about it later she said it was probably delayed shock. Now that I was looking after two young children, instead of just one, the tremor got much worse and sometimes I felt too embarrassed about it to go out. I found myself snapping at the pair of them all day long, and sometimes I put Neil to bed as early as five-thirty in the evening just to have energy for Janette. I felt guilty about it but it was the only way I could manage. On those occasions I thought perhaps dad had been right and I should have stopped at one child. Seeing I was so run-down, the medical staff again urged me to send Janette away for a time. They thought I wasn't trying hard enough to get her using her rockers and that I needed expert help. Neil was now six months old and Janette wasn't going to get any more jealous, so I agreed. She was to be taught to walk at Marple Children's Hospital near Buxton in Derbyshire, where the Cripples' Help Society had a special school. It was the first and last time Terry showed an interest in her by offering to take her there by taxi.

I don't think I could have taken her to Buxton myself and walked away. It wasn't so much that Janette was disturbed at the thought of parting – it was me who was upset! In fact Janette seemed excited to be going somewhere special where they'd teach her to move around without her potty. I felt that the whole purpose of my life was about to vanish and tears poured out of my eyes as Terry left with her. I should have consoled myself with thoughts of how exasperating she was, but all I could think of was her bad-tempered red curly hair and how much I loved her.

It was about this time that Terry's mother decided to put up a photograph of Janette in her living-room. I'd had it taken when she was ten months old, wearing her cosmetic arms and looking much like any other toddler. She had a white frilly dress and rosy cheeks and I enjoyed puzzling over Mrs Henry's likely reaction when visitors admired her pretty grand-daughter. I don't think she felt any differently about Janette but perhaps she hoped she could pass her off as a normal child.

I made sure I visited Marple at least once a week, even though it was a fair trek by train and bus. It was on a hillside in the most beautiful countryside and the air was really bracing, especially in the winter. Terry didn't visit Janette once but dad usually came with me and we'd leave Neil with a baby-sitter. I didn't think it was fair to take him and have Janette watch us both disappear down the drive at the end of the day. Not that I had to worry about her because she was happy from the moment she arrived at Marple and showed no signs of wanting to leave. That was just as well because she was so stubborn that even the experts needed time to make her walk with her artificial legs. In fact she would do nothing they asked her and they were beginning to think it was a hopeless task and that she might just as well come home, when there was a breakthrough. Janette had been left alone in the ward listening to one of her favourite records by the Beatles. She was infuriated when it got stuck in a groove on "Love me do . . . me do . . . me do . . . me do . . . " If anyone had been there she'd have demanded instant action to make her beloved Beatles sing properly again but in the absence of a willing adult she was forced to do something about it herself. She rocked from side to side till she reached the other end of the ward where the record player was kept and, with one last violent rocking motion, jerked the record into play. The nurse who walked into the room moments later described her expression as triumphant.

Chapter 4

CALIE

With Janette away in hospital and only one small child to look after, my life became much easier. It was almost like being an ordinary mother for the first time with a baby who attracted smiles in the street rather than awkward glances. It also meant I could go out to work to help buy a few extras and pay for the journeys to Marple. Every night of the week between 8 p.m. and 2 a.m., while dad looked after Neil, I served behind the bar at Tiffany's, a new club in the centre of Manchester. I made friends with another girl at the club called Lorraine and she kept asking me to go out on the town with her. "All you ever do is work," she said. "Surprise us all. Come out and have a good time!"

So the next Saturday we went to the Blue Bell club in Lloyd Street, a mysterious place I'd never been to before. It was very dark and the only light was on stage where a steel band was bonging away. I'd had a drink, which cost me an evening's work at Tiffany's, and was on the floor dancing with a fellow I'd just met when I felt these big brown eyes staring out at me from the back row of the band. A broad-shouldered guy on the bass pans had me fixed in his gaze and it was like being plugged into an electric charge. I carried on dancing till the music stopped but I'd lost interest in whoever it was I was dancing with. At the interval I'd just sat down with Lorraine when the black musician came over to our table. He was six foot three to my five foot, and light skinned with a pointed nose and gorgeous melting eyes. He turned out to be a friend of Lorraine's – "her bit of spare" as she put it later. She said his dad was Lord Mayor of Barbados, and that he was friendly with the Lancashire cricket team. He asked her straightaway to introduce us and that's when I first heard the name Calie.

There were to be many times when I wished he'd simply stayed in my mind as the nameless man from the back of the band.

"'Struth, he doesn't half fancy you!" whispered Lorraine in the ladies'. We'd gone to powder our noses while the band was getting ready for the second half. Looking in the mirror, I couldn't help feeling a touch of vanity. I had slanting dark eyes and high cheekbones and sometimes people told me I looked a bit like Elizabeth Taylor. I don't remember anything else until the club threw us all out at about half past two in the morning. Calie then insisted on taking us home and he led us to a battered blue van which the band used for all its gear. I made sure Lorraine and I sat together in the front, but of course he managed to drop her off first and when I tried getting out with her, he grabbed hold of my arm. As Lorraine called cheerily "See you tomorrow!" I hissed at her not to leave me on my own – I had visions of him taking me off to eat me – but she pretended not to hear. He kept asking when he could see me again but, although the attraction was mutual, I felt embarrassed and just avoided the question. When we got near home, I asked him to let me out a couple of streets away in case any of the neighbours saw me. It was bad enough coming home so late but in those days nobody went out with a black man and I knew if word got round to my dad all hell would be let loose.

About a week later I was leaving Tiffany's when who should I see outside but Calie in his van. He took me to a pub for a drink and I have to confess it was the early hours of the morning before I got home to Gordon Avenue – in fact I think it was dawn. From then on me and Calie were together most nights and it put me in a difficult position with dad. I could either move out altogether or bring Calie home, which on balance I thought would hurt dad more. He had enough to cope with already as mum was very ill by this time. As well as treating her family like total strangers, and offering her purse to everyone she met in the street, she was often very aggressive and we had to make sure Neil was kept well away from her. I used this as an excuse when I told dad I was moving into a flat, where there was a woman who'd look after Neil while I was at work.

I found a suitable place not far from Gordon Avenue, but as soon as the landlord realised my boyfriend was coloured, he made it quite clear that I couldn't stay. Now I was really out of my depth. I didn't know any of the mixed-race areas in Manchester and when Calie told me he'd got a flat for us in Old Trafford, he might just as well have been saying he was taking me to Siberia, not somewhere half a mile away. I was absolutely devastated when we moved in. It wasn't a flat at all but a room. There was a bed, a cupboard, and a paraffin heater which made the whole place stink. There were bare floorboards and the curtains were too small for the one window. The house was owned by a man from Calie's work and his wife, Vicky, and we had the use of their kitchen and bathroom. It was like nothing that I'd been used to, but at least with Neil's cot and his toys it looked a bit more homely.

If ever I felt angry that Calie had brought me to this alien home on the wrong side of Manchester, I comforted myself by thinking how kind he was to Neil. He'd spend hours playing with the child and never minded looking after him when I went to Tiffany's. He also made sure I visited Janette regularly and he tried very hard to make friends with her when she came home to Manchester for the weekend. She was having a fine old time at Marple where she was the only child with such severe disabilities and always the centre of attention. Most of the other kids had common complaints like dislocated hips and they were all ages from six months to five years old. At night they slept in wards of high-sided cots and during the day they played in a nursery. The staff adored Janette. They said she put so much expression in that cheeky freckled face that to watch her was constant entertainment. Mind you, she was very naughty and still demanding, and when she got cross she had a terrible habit of head-butting, "Sticking the nut" on you, we called it. She did it one day at home to Neil and for a couple of seconds I thought he was concussed. She hadn't grown any fonder of Neil actually, and I still left him at home when I went to visit her. She didn't like Calie either at first and preferred to have me all to herself. But she didn't cry when I left – she just gave me a long list of the toys she wanted me to bring next time.

I must admit I was enjoying my freedom, and my new social life with Calie. I was twenty-two with a lot of living ahead of me and whereas I'd been used to being home by ten thirty at night, now it was ten thirty before my day got started. I'd go to the pub first and then onto Tiffany's and after Tiffany's I'd be off with Calie. He knocked me off my feet with his attentions and when I was with him I never encountered any prejudice. People seemed to admire him, perhaps because he was so handsome. He was a three-piece-suit man, very distinguished and with charming manners. And his band the Royals carried quite a bit of kudos. I used to go with them when they played at golf clubs and dinner dances, and I was always treated with respect. One night I went with them to Ross-on-Wye where some bigwig was having a special do. The atmosphere was too formal and stiff at first, and I ended up putting on a long dress and dancing to get people warmed up. It was so successful I started doing it regularly after that. Sometimes I even joined the boys on stage, playing the maracas.

All the Royals became friends of mine, though some of them seemed a bit wary of Calie. He was always coming up with grand ideas and promises of important bookings that would make their fortunes overnight. I noticed that, though the others seemed willing to play along with him, they never put any money up front and at first I thought they were taking liberties. It was only much later that I discovered what the rest of the band had learned the hard way – you could never trust Calie with any cash. Sometimes, someone in the band would get a bit too friendly when Calie's back was turned, but never George, a serious-minded man from St Kitts who was always polite but held himself somewhat aloof. He was a welder and very hard-working, and he clearly disapproved of Calie and his flashy ways.

One of my favourite songs the Royals played was about love being blind, which in my case was perfectly true because there was certainly a lot that I just didn't see. Then one day, my eyes were opened. I came back to our dingy little room in Trafford one night and had just put on my housecoat when Vicky knocked on the door and said there was someone waiting to see me. A scruffy looking woman, dressed in a mackintosh with a scarf over her head, was standing in the hall. She was white like me and she had three small half-caste children in tow. I recognised one of them at once. Calie had told me he had a five-year-old daughter, Laura, by a former girlfriend and she'd even come to visit us one Saturday. Here she was, in the hallway, with two baby sisters and a mother who was clearly more than a passing fancy from Calie's past. I think I guessed right away what she was going to tell me, that she was his wife, Julie, and I felt sorry for her. She blurted out, "I've come scruffy because I know for a fact he'll have told you that's why he's not with me. I'm not a showpiece and he's ashamed of me. He thinks I'm dirty and shabby and don't look after the kids properly." Then she told me she was pregnant again. I was trying to explain that I hadn't known Calie was married when he came flying in and started pushing her out of the room towards the front door. I screamed at him to leave her alone but he went on kicking and shoving her and I couldn't bear to watch. Upstairs I lay on the bed sobbing my heart out. I'd have left him right away but the cunning bastard had taken the keys from my bag. In the end I must have cried myself to sleep but I woke in the early hours of the morning with Calie trying to sneak into bed beside me. Somehow he got round me. He said he'd been separated from Julie for a long time and had nothing to do with her now, and I felt it had to be true because whenever I was out he was at home looking after Neil.

I tried to put Calie's wife out of my mind but I kept thinking about how I'd broken up her family and I wanted to make amends. Once I started asking questions I found that a lot of people knew about her but they'd been told to keep it quiet. I soon learned where she lived – in Moss Side – and I went to find her and tell her I was going to leave Calie. Then I went back to Gordon Avenue.

I'd managed to keep Calie a secret from dad, who was delighted to have me and Neil back home again. Poor mum was too far gone to know what was happening. She was so ill that we had to take her to Manchester Royal Infirmary and it was then that they diagnosed pre-senile dementia and told us she'd be better off in a psychiatric hospital. Dad couldn't face the thought of letting her go. He said he'd be ashamed not to stand by her after all these years. So she came home for a while but every day she seemed to get worse. I'd come in to find the kitchen filled with gas because she'd turned all the rings on without lighting them, and we were frightened she'd do some real damage to herself. So reluctantly dad and I had to certify her and a nurse came to take her away in a limousine with tinted windows. We travelled with her to Prestwich, the old lunatic asylum on the road to Bury. There were rows of ugly brick buildings set in acres of land, separated by winding roads and trees, and it was bitterly cold. Inside, you could hear people groaning and screaming, and there was the smell of incontinence. When we led mum in through the gates, we knew she'd never come out but, and I suppose this was cowardly, we told her she was only there to be assessed. We left her on the reception ward with a box of chocolates and a locker-full of familiar possessions and walked out with tears streaming down our faces.

I'd been staying with dad for about a week when he came in from work one night and said that there was a funny man hanging about at the end of Gordon Avenue. "Every time I come home there's a shadowy figure but he keeps diving into the Labour Exchange at the bottom of the road!" Well I knew it was Calie because I'd seen him myself, but I wasn't going to say anything till I had to. Then on the next Saturday we had mum home for the weekend and dad was out shopping when who should turn up at the door but Calie. Mum started offering him tea and biscuits and I stood there begging him to leave. "I'm not going anywhere without you," he said. I told him I felt like the scum of the earth and didn't want his broken marriage on my conscience. I was trying to get him out of the house and mum was hovering at my elbow, offering him pieces of pie and hot drinks and chatting on about what lovely weather it was, even though it was pissing with rain outside, when dad walked in. Of course he put two and two together immediately and started calling me every name under the sun. Then he put his arm round mum's waist and told me to get out of his house and never come back.

Calie was waiting outside when I emerged about half an hour later with Neil and a bag of belongings. I think he felt more secure after that, knowing I couldn't keep running home to my daddy. We talked for hours about his wife and his kids and how he'd kept his marriage a secret because he was afraid to lose me, and yes she was having another baby but he didn't think it was his. I loved him enough to believe him and we settled back into our old ways. At that time he was working as a crane driver at Trafford Park but he would often come home or take days off, and after about six months he stopped working. It meant we could stay longer in bed together and that suited us both. To be honest, sleeping with Terry had been a bit boring, but with Calie it was the real thing – a passionate love affair. He was kind and considerate in a way Terry had never been, and when we went out together he always seemed so proud of me. I was besotted with the man, and some nights I couldn't bring myself to leave him. I started missing shifts at Tiffany's and the manager got fed up with me and gave me the sack. One thing led to another and it wasn't long before we got badly into debt.

Things got so bad that although we always had enough to feed Neil, I was beginning to wonder where my next meal was coming from. This was when Calie made his suggestion. Why, he said, didn't I go out and earn some money on the streets. Lots of his friends' wives and girlfriends did the same and it would quickly get us out of our financial difficulties. At first I was shocked rigid. The nearest I'd ever come to prostitutes was in the centre of Manchester in the shopping arcades. I remember being fascinated as a child by the women who stood inside Lewis's Arcade with chains round their ankles, and saying to my mum, "I want a dress like that pretty lady's." Well she went totally berserk. "You don't look at that kind of person," she said in a tone of disgust, dragging me away. Later when I was at school, one or two of the girls were said to be going down Moss Side on the game and I felt a mixture of revulsion and pity, certain that it would never happen to me. But now, at the great age of twenty-three, I wasn't so certain about anything. I'd already cut myself off from my family and childhood friends by living with a black man. If that wasn't enough of a stigma, doing what Calie suggested couldn't make me sink much lower. Strange as it must seem, it never occurred to me that he didn't love me, though I couldn't understand how someone normally so possessive and jealous could let me go with other men. When I put this to him, he explained that what I'd be doing was different. He told me how to make a man so excited that sexual intercourse didn't have to take place. After about a fortnight I was worn down by all his coaxing and tempted by his talk of us buying a house together. But what finally made me give in was his kindness to Neil. He went downstairs one teatime and came back with a bowl of rice – all that was left for us to eat. Neither he nor I had a mouthful. Neil of course ate the lot and I thought that if he could do that for my baby then the least I could do was go out and earn some money.

It was five o'clock on a cold November evening when Calie took me the short distance to Withington Road, a notorious red-light district. I was wearing a three-quarter-length astra-khan coat with a fur collar, over a very short black jersey-wool dress, black patent leather shoes and a pair of black gloves. My hair was back-combed into a bouffant and I was wearing my normal make-up – just a discreet amount. I didn't look a bit like the other girls and I felt totally out of place. Calie dropped me off at the corner of Burford Road, where the rows of shops give way to red-brick houses. Before leaving me there, he went into a chemist's and bought me a packet of Durex. That added to my panic because I'd never even seen them before. Then he told me to keep walking up and down the road because otherwise I'd be picked up by the police, and he left me. I'd gone barely a few yards from the shops when a van pulled over. I froze, feeling sick in my stomach, thinking "Oh Lord! this is it, this is the moment! What am I going to say to this man?" I heard the van stop and I had to force myself to turn round, only to find myself staring into an all too familiar face. I don't know whether it was relief or shame I felt, or disgust, but it was Viv at the wheel, one of Calie's best mates from the band. "Sheila, what in God's name are you doing here? Don't you know what kind of place this is?" As I made some feeble excuse about going to the chemist to buy cough medicine for the baby, he bundled me into the van and drove me straight back to Calie.

As soon as Viv was out of sight, Calie started bawling me out for being such a fool and in half an hour he had me back on Withington Road. He'd given me instructions: not to go with black men or Indians, not to get into a car that was old and battered, not to enter into arguments about money. He said I was to ask for five pounds even though we were working a two-pound area. When my first genuine client came along, a middle-aged Greek in a big blue Vauxhall, I named my price and after a moment's hesitation he said, "Oh all right, then. You do look a cut above the rest of the girls round here." He could tell how green I was and I think he took a bit of a shine to me because he took me into a pub for a drink and ended up paying me fifteen pounds. Like the idiot I was, I gave him my real name instead of inventing one as the other girls did, and I told him I was working to pay for my baby boy. I never brought Janette into the conversation. He was called Ari and he remained one of my clients all the time I was on the game. He owned a club in town and he used to take me there and treat me like his girlfriend.

Calie was really pleased with the money I brought home that night. Out of a packet of condoms, I'd used one and thrown the other two away so he'd think I'd had three clients. He could smell the drink on my breath but I said I'd had to go into a pub to get away from a roving policeman and he believed me. The next night wasn't so easy. I think I made one fiver but another client knocked me down to two pounds telling me to come back when I was more experienced. The punters in Withington Road were a mixed bunch but, keeping to Calie's rules, I managed to avoid trouble and I never earned less than seventy-five pounds a week which was a lot of money in 1964.

Chapter 5

THE LONG BAR

Late in the afternoon, Calie would drop me off at the far end of Withington Road where it was quiet and more often than not I'd be picked up before I got to the church. There was only one night when I gave up without doing any business, and that was when the vice squad was on the prowl. Mostly I stayed with the punter in his car, down a side-street, and I found that Calie was right when he said the whole thing was usually over and done with before you reached intercourse. I was also lucky with my Greek friend. Ari would take me out each week, paying generously for me to dress up smartly and provide him with companionship as much as anything. I'd only been on Withington Road about four weeks when he advised me to go more up-market, and helped me to find a flat about ten minutes away in Didsbury. I'd pick up a punter and get to the flat and back again in three-quarters of an hour. It was on the third floor of a block occupied mainly by business people, and only the cleaner knew what I was doing. We never spoke about it but she always made sure I had plenty of clean linen.

Gradually there were more and more evenings when I didn't have to go out of the flat at all. I had a telephone and clients could ring up for an appointment. I always put on nice clothes and I dyed my hair red and kept it at shoulder length. I was beginning to enjoy my success and the money it brought in.

I may still have been as daft as a brush over Calie, but I was at least getting wiser to his faults. He had a nasty temper and jealousy was usually the cause. He couldn't bear it if any man except a punter took any interest in me and if I threatened to leave him he'd give me a good hiding. But he'd always try to make up for it afterwards. He'd fuss around, make me cups of tea, and if that didn't work he only had to lure me into the bedroom to win me back. I also knew that he was gambling away most of the money I earned for him. Usually it was the horses but he was the sort who'd bet on what time it would stop raining. At first I was fool enough to let Calie have my night's earnings and wait for him to give me some back. I used to put the money in a kitchen drawer, jumbled up with things like paper bags, string and bottle-openers. Calie took what he wanted, which was usually most of it but gradually I got wiser and put three-quarters of the money in the drawer and kept what was left for myself. Then I cut it down to fifty-fifty. I never told him about the flat or that most of my clients were wealthy businessmen. Many of them seemed happy to be with me as an escort, to dinner dances or clubs, instead of for the more traditional purpose. They were so keen for me to go with them that, whenever I had the nerve to say that I hadn't a thing to wear at their posh outings, they'd give me the money to buy a really smart dress or coat.

Most of them were decent men who played golf on Sundays, ran their lives as they wanted them and took their wives on foreign holidays once a year. They all said that they loved their wives but complained that there was no sex-life in their marriages. I used to hear that a lot and began to realise it was a load of old cobblers. There was plenty of sex left in those marriages – it was just that the men wanted it with other women. They needed to feel wanted, which was pretty easy for me, being an affectionate type and once I got to know them I could be genuinely loving. They said that I made them feel special, even if it was just for half an hour. And there was one man I got particularly fond of. He was Jewish and owned one of Manchester's large retail stores, and we saw each other two or three times a week. He was good company, even if he did blame me for getting his wife pregnant! It was when Neil was sick one day and I couldn't meet him. It was that night, he said afterwards, that his wife conceived and he joked about calling the baby Sheila.

There were a few, of course, who weren't so pleasant. They'd call me over to the car and ask whether I did this or that for money, and then drive off having got their kicks. Or a man would ask me if he could look at my bust and the first time I was so naïve I opened my coat, giving him a cheap eye-full and doing myself out of some money. I'm still not sure why I seemed to be so successful on the game, especially as I was very straightlaced really. Some of the girls on Withington Road seemed to relish oral sex or bondage but I could never have managed anything like that, and I always insisted that the punters wore rubbers.

Thanks to Ari I soon put the Withington Road evenings well behind me. Once I'd established myself in the Didsbury flat, he introduced me to the Long Bar, a really plush rendez-vous on the corner of Oxford Road and Great Bridgewater Street. It had a striking curved front with two entrances. The Long Bar was home to two types of girl. There was one class who stood outside and fought for the best pitch, while the other sat inside at the tables, on view to the customers as they strolled in and wandered up to the bar. I was one of the inside girls and I'd sit smoking as cool as I could manage with a glass of lemonade or a coke. It was a nice place to be but the waiting always made me feel rather self-consciously like being in a cattle market. The waiters would bring messages over, sometimes with their own cheeky comments thrown in, and they got good tips from the punters. Fortunately I hardly ever got through a whole glass before being picked up and it was here I met some of my best clients. It was a great bonus having a smart flat to take them back to.

Of course, there were some people I'd rather not have met, and I lived in constant anxiety from the risk of seeing people I knew. But the shock of my life came one night when I saw my dad walk down the steps and into the bar. Luckily the lights were kept very low, and with my head down I rushed straight out of the other entrance and across the road to Mick's café. I waited long enough for dad to have a drink, find what he was looking for, and leave. It was upsetting seeing him there but I could well understand why he needed the comfort of the Long Bar. Besides, I was in no position to pass judgement. I was leading two lives which I kept completely separate. During the day I was Neil's mum. In the evening I was on the game.

Saturday was a good night for clients but on Sundays I'd visit mum in Prestwich or go and see Janette.

By the time Janette was nearly three the scandal of thalidomide was well and truly out in the open, though I can't say I'd taken much notice of newspaper reports about the drug and its tragic effects. Apparently a Professor Smithells, a doctor at Alder Hey Children's Hospital in Liverpool, had been keeping a register of babies born in the area with deformities. When it became clear thalidomide was the cause, he decided to set up a special unit at Alder Hey for the children and he contacted parents on his register. For some reason Janette wasn't on this register and we only heard about the special unit from the hospital at Marple. Janette was only a tot, light enough to carry around, and she must have been sorry to leave her friends at Marple but she accepted the move with her usual stoicism. We went in a Manchester ambulance but had to get out at the Merseyside border and transfer to a Liverpool ambulance for the rest of the journey to Knotty Ash. The unit was a bungalow next to the main hospital and I'll never forget walking in and seeing so many other children like Janette, all in the same room. Some were shuffling around on the floor, one was barging around on rockers with a crash helmet on his head, another had a paint-brush between her teeth. Now, for the first time, I realised what people meant when they talked about thalidomide and I wondered what monsters could have invented a drug to produce deformed limbs like these. Some of the guilt I'd felt about being the cause of Janette's handicap started to drift away now that I had proof it was the pills which were to blame, though I suppose it never disappeared altogether because it was me who'd swallowed the frigging things. "Good God," I thought, "at least Janette's not on her own. And these kids must belong to somebody which means I'm not on my own, either." As for Janette, she summed it all up in a moment, told everyone who she was as bold as brass and joined in with the games.

The unit was officially opened a few months later by Group Captain Douglas Bader, who'd lost his legs in a flying accident. Janette was chosen to present him with some golf-clubs and I felt so proud as she wobbled her way over to him on her rockers. The staff at Alder Hey were wonderful. Janette wasn't too pleased with them, though, when they fitted her with gas-powered arms. These were heavy metal contraptions strapped to her chest with a cylinder for the air and ugly claws for hands. She operated them by moving her shoulders but it was a painstaking process and she could do everything twice as fast without them. Most of the other children had at least got tiny arms and it gave them a huge advantage. The other difference between her and most of the children was that they lived in the Liverpool area and went home at night, but she had to stay on a general ward in the main hospital. In her usual fashion, though, she made lots of friends and admirers and never seemed to feel hard done by. When I went to see her I always had to spend hours being taken round the wards to meet a growing band of patients and nurses. I had more contact with them than with the other thalidomide parents, who were in and out of the unit on weekdays collecting their children. I didn't have much chance to meet them so never got drawn into the early stages of the campaign for compensation. In fact it never occurred to me to ask for money for what had happened. I hadn't even registered Janette as disabled, and didn't do so till she was eleven years old. Although I may have been streetwise, I didn't have a clue about officials, offices and forms and so on. It wasn't part of my upbringing to ask the government for money and I think everyone else took it for granted Sheila could stand on her own two feet.

It was easier for me to go to Liverpool at weekends than for Janette to come to the room I shared with Calie in Manchester. I knew she was getting the best possible care at Alder Hey, with experts who knew all there was to know by now about thalidomide children. Of course I wanted to bring her home, but home to what? You would hardly describe my lifestyle as stable and although I could ask people to look after Neil while I was out and about, I could hardly expect them to have a disabled youngster as well.

When I wasn't on the game I was trying to be a good mum to Neil, who was now a lively toddler, and I also wanted to spend as much time as possible with Calie. I enjoyed the company of his friends in the band and we had a much better social life than Terry and me ever had. But it left little time for travelling to Alder Hey and my visits became less frequent than they should have been. I knew that dad was going there once a week without fail, but I didn't manage much more than a visit a month. To make up for it, I always arrived laden with presents – puzzles and books and clothes. I felt terribly guilty but Janette never seemed resentful. I think she put me on some sort of pedestal. I was her glamorous mummy and she was always glad to see me and keen to show me off to the other kids. After a couple of close shaves, I started coming in the middle of the week to avoid meeting dad, but one day I bumped into him at Alder Hey. I was sitting with Janette outside the bungalow when he appeared. He was obviously looking forward to seeing his plucky little granddaughter, and giving her some sweets he'd brought along, when he found me there as well. His face went tight with anger and he said, "If I had a knife on me, I'd stick it in you!"

"Don't you talk to my mummy like that," piped up Janette and suddenly he looked crumpled and tired. I felt ashamed because it was really him Janette should have stuck up for, not me. He was a better father than her own, and much better than her mother. I ran out of the hospital garden in tears, leaving Janette with her grandad.

But my guilt turned to anger some months later when I discovered that dad was encouraging a Welsh couple to adopt Janette. I'd often heard her talk about Uncle Glyn and Auntie Edie. They were the parents of the boy in the next bed on her ward. He was in Alder Hey suffering from diabetes and whenever they visited him they'd come and speak to Janette as well. Even when he got better and went home, they carried on visiting her and for a while I was glad she was getting the extra attention. Then one day she told me she'd been with her grandad to visit Uncle Glyn in Wales and I really hit the roof. I stormed into the matron's office and swore that if she ever let Janette go off to strangers again without asking me, I'd complain to the head of the hospital and make sure she never worked again.

I knew that I was being an unreasonable little bitch, because I wasn't exactly the perfect mother, but what they were doing struck me in my tenderest spot and I had no defence. I half thought while I was raging against them that I should have let them all get on with it. If anyone had asked my permission I'd probably have given it, but no-one had thought to consult me. When the matron had calmed me down, I told them that Janette could go out with the Welsh family so long as I was informed. The matron sensibly asked, "What if we can't get hold of you in time?" So, because I didn't want to deprive Janette in any way, I gave her a letter of authorisation. By now even the matron was confused. She must have thought I was mad, complaining hysterically one moment and writing a helpful letter the next, but I was Janette's mum and I wanted that to be clear.

I met Glyn and Edie at the hospital one day. They were a gentle middle-class couple with three sons. He had a business of his own and she looked rather homely and did voluntary work. I think they were surprised to see that I wasn't quite the scarlet ogre I'd been painted by dad, but an ordinary twenty-five year old trying to make some sort of life for my family. They gave me a lift to the station and on the way I said, "I do know that you want my daughter and I'm telling you now that I have no objections to you visiting her and I'm very grateful for it and for the presents you bring her. I don't mind if you take her to your home but as regards adoption, forget it." It was then Glyn told me that adoption hadn't been their idea. It was my father who'd suggested it because he said he was worried about Janette's future if anything happened to him. After all I'd been through, Glyn and Edie left me at the station feeling rather small.

I made up my mind while I was waiting for the train that I'd do everything I possibly could to get Janette home for good. When I told Janette on my next visit she said, "My grandad said I might be going to live at Uncle Glyn's." "Did he?" I replied. "Well you can tell your grandad from me there's no way you're going to live with Uncle Glyn and Auntie Edie! Your home is with me."

The first step in bringing this about was to get a suitable place to live, and I badgered the council silly till they shut me up with a four-bedroomed house in Wythenshawe. By this time I was in the process of divorcing Terry – at last – and Neil, Janette and I had taken Calie's name by deed poll. I'd discovered that I was expecting Calie's baby, so we were now well and truly the Mottley family. But before we were ready to have Janette home there was still a lot to be done. I thought it was important to earn as much money as possible until I'd had this next baby. After that I planned to come off the game.

It was around this time that I learned other parents of thalidomide children were fighting for compensation from Distillers. Altogether there were four hundred and fifty-six babies born in Britain with various degrees of thalidomide deformities. Some parents grouped together to form the Society for the Aid of Thalidomide Children, a registered charity which eventually had about four hundred members, though I wasn't one of them. They got some help from the wife of the Lord Mayor of London, Lady Hoare, who helped raise stacks of money under the Lady Hoare Thalidomide Appeal. I got to hear about this when someone called Mrs Jarvis came round and started mithering me about applying for financial help, but for several reasons I resisted the idea. I didn't see why I should have to use my child to get what I wanted out of life. It was bad enough giving birth to someone with Janette's deformities without exploiting her and getting money out of her. It wasn't in my nature to go moaning on about having a child with no arms and no legs, as if looking for sympathy. I started to read here and there about some parents suing Distillers for negligence, but it didn't seem the sort of thing that I could do, especially as Mrs Jarvis kept saying that Distillers was a huge company that hadn't even admitted liability and wasn't budging an inch. Besides, I didn't give a toss for any compensation. But Mrs Jarvis kept coming round and droning on about it, so to shut her up I told her to send me her forms. When they came, I stuffed them in a drawer and forgot about them. My life was complicated enough and I didn't want to get involved.

I wanted to prepare Janette for the day when she could come home for good, so I started to fetch her on occasional weekends. She didn't have a bed of her own at first and she had to share my double bed. Calie would sneak in on the other side and she'd tell him, "Don't you put your arm round my mummy!" Neil had always called Calie "Daddy" – in fact he was saying daddy before he learned to say mummy – but Janette would reduce him to tears in seconds. "He's not your daddy, you know," she'd say, "so don't call him that!" Eventually she got used to Calie, though I think she always resented his place in the family. Surprisingly, though, she was very excited when I told her I was going to have another baby.

I was glad to be having a child by Calie and hoped desperately that it would be a girl. The two babies I'd lost had both been girls and then there was Janette. I'd proved I could have a normal healthy baby with Neil but I think I'd have gone on trying till I got a perfectly formed daughter, one that I could dress up and take to ballet classes as my mum had taken me when I was a child. I fantasised about a little girl with ribbons in her hair, a short dress, frilly knickers and a pair of red shoes. Luckily it was a very easy pregnancy and I was still working when I was five and a half months gone. Apart from a slightly bigger tummy than normal, it didn't show. I was eight stone and could still get in to size ten mini-skirts. I always kept myself smart, spending an hour every morning in the hairdresser's in Oxford Road. One evening I'd been with a client at my flat and was waiting for a taxi to take me back to the Long Bar. The taxi rank was opposite St Mary's Hospital where I'd had Janette and Neil and I was just about to get into a cab when I collapsed. The driver took me straight into casualty. I was haemorrhaging and went into labour but a doctor gave me tablets to stop it. They kept me in for three weeks and then called Calie in. They were worried about internal bleeding and weren't sure if they could save both me and the baby. To be honest, at that stage I was so tired and disappointed that I don't think I cared much about saving the baby. But Calie was concerned to keep both of us and hung around anxiously while they set about inducing labour. After all the waiting, they went into crash action and Hayley was born, weighing three pounds and two ounces, a pathetic scrag of a thing with very dark colouring, curly black hair and her father's beautiful eyes.

I phoned Janette the same day. Her favourite member of staff, Mrs Smith, brought her to the phone for me to tell her the news. "I've got a baby sister!" she screeched at the top of her voice and Mrs Smith took the phone and said she was dancing all over the place in spite of her continuing fear of the rockers.

Hayley was in the premature-baby unit for four months. Although she was the perfect little girl I'd longed for, it was difficult to form the instant bond that had been there with both Janette and Neil. Perhaps that was because all I had to put my arms round was an incubator. Calie was thrilled to bits though and he'd come and dote over her, pestering the nurses with questions about how much weight she was putting on and when she could come home. Although I'd planned to give up work when she was born, I hated the idea of making do on social security when there was a ready income at hand and I was soon back on the game. Between clients at the flat I'd fit in visits to St Mary's to breast-feed my lovely Hayley.

Chapter 6

THE GAME ENDS

One summer evening I was just leaving the Long Bar with a rather tasty punter when a policeman stopped me. "It's all right mate, she's with me," said my client, trying to get me off the hook. But then the copper asked if he'd come to court to testify to that effect, and naturally enough he backed off. My first court appearance was a few days later and I was fined for soliciting. In the next few weeks I got picked up twice more and had to fork out more money. Big cool Calie was really shaken by this. He was afraid he'd be caught for pimping and decided it wasn't safe to spend every night in our Wythenshawe house. This was when he started to stay away for days at a time, and I soon discovered that he was going to Julie, his wife. It left me with a problem of finding someone to look after Neil and Hayley while I was out earning. Fortunately a neighbour introduced me to a girl called Anne who had two small children and needed some money, so she came to mind them. She was quite tall, with long black hair, and she was the kind of person who'd always do you a good turn if she could. If I was working long hours, Anne would come and stay overnight and she and I became good friends.

I'd also ganged up with a couple of girls in the Long Bar with similar backgrounds to my own. They were from decent homes but somehow mixed up with one guy or another who scared them enough to keep them working the bars for a living. I could have done all my business from the flat but kept going to the Long Bar for the companionship. It was over two years since I'd been introduced to prostitution and I was nicely established. I had my days for working and my days for being home with the kids. But in some ways I was still very naïve. When Calie came round and told me I had to come with him to St Luke's, I hugged him for thinking about Hayley's christening. "Not St Luke's the church, you booby!" he said. "St Luke's the clap clinic." I'd caught VD off him, and while I was still breast-feeding. If it wasn't humiliating enough to be going to the clinic, I discovered that Julie had got it as well and we were both attending St Luke's on different days. That was the last straw. I got the police to chuck him out and I threw all his belongings onto the street after him.

That should have been the end of it and it would have been – if only I could have kept Calie in the living-room. I could hold my own with him there but Calie ruthlessly exploited my weakness for him in the bedroom. He was a handsome bastard. He was also a wonderful father to the kids. Neil in particular adored him. Besides, I couldn't exactly avoid meeting him because we both wanted to visit Hayley who was back in hospital with bronchitis. As we sat over the cot he held my hand and I agreed to take him back, but on my terms. I'd work so many days a week and no more, and I'd do what I wanted, not what he demanded.

I think by now I was determined to make myself do without him and everything he did strengthened my resolve. The Christmas after Hayley was born he went walkabout with my turkey money. I'd done all the shopping before Christmas Eve except for the turkey. Calie offered to buy one while he was in the city centre and I gave him all the money in my purse, but he didn't come back for a week. In the meantime of course we had to make do with stew on Christmas Day. Strangely it was Terry who turned up instead. We'd all met up in court several months earlier. I'd been taking out an affiliation order against Calie for Hayley, and Terry was up for failing to pay his maintenance for Janette and Neil. The magistrate sent Terry to prison for six months and Calie, who'd never set eyes on him before, took pity on him and followed him down to the cells. Then he went off to the shops to buy Terry cigarettes to start his sentence with, and after that the two of them became firm chums. I wouldn't be surprised if they didn't swop notes and start ganging up against me! That was when Calie gave Terry our address and invited him round when he'd done his bird at Christmas. As it turned out, Calie wasn't there to greet him, but I was glad of the company and touched that he'd bought presents for all the kids – a carpenter's set for Neil, a xylophone for Janette, who was now four, and a toy duck for the baby.

In the following year, 1967, Janette left the thalidomide unit at Alder Hey and went to a residential school called Margaret Barclay School, which was in the countryside around Liverpool. Several of her friends from the unit went too and they were all very proud to be at a proper school. Now that she was five and old enough to understand, I tried to explain why she was different from able-bodied children. I said it was my fault really because I'd been give some tablets by the doctor to stop me being sick and these had damaged her in the womb. I took great care to give her the exact truth and afterwards she looked at me and said, "I don't think it was your fault, mummy. I don't think it was anybody's fault really." And that is how Janette's always been, always accepting the way things are for her. Only once, years later, did she turn on me and blame me for taking those tablets.

It was in 1967 that some thalidomide parents were due to meet Distillers in court to bring their case of negligence. But then Distillers agreed to settle the case out of court. They accepted a forty per cent liability for damages in exchange for the parents dropping their claims. To my amazement, the parents' solicitors, Kimber Bull, recommended accepting this offer instead of telling them where they could stuff it! But the parents weren't having any of that and told Distillers where they could get off, so the whole messy business was delayed yet again.

Of course all this hardly meant anything to me, let alone Janette. She was a lovable, happy-go-lucky child, always laughing, but just as demanding as ever. I worried about that sometimes because I knew that when she came home she'd have to take her place as part of the family. Her teachers thought the world of her and wherever she went she seemed to be the centre of attention. I think she was probably cleverer than the other kids. She was reading to herself by the time she was six years old. She was very attached to her first teacher,

Mrs O'Neil, a kindly silver-haired woman who let her paint and read to her heart's content. After a while, though, she became rather frustrated and bored at Margaret Barclay and about the only thing she always enjoyed was going to feed Alfie, the donkey who lived in a field near the school. And she was thrilled when it was time for the school play *The Ugly Duckling* and Mrs O'Neil chose her to be mother duck. I went along, of course, only to find that Janette had caught measles and was stuck in bed. We stayed in the dormitory, listening to the cheerful sounds of the play going on below, and the poor child sobbed her heart out. She cried again at the end of the school holiday when it was time to leave home and go back to Margaret Barclay. I wasn't used to Janette being homesick and it was hard putting her in the mini-van and watching it drive away.

The other children were also having their ups and downs. Neil had turned from a placid toddler into a right tearaway. He delighted in winding me up and he was a bit of a wanderer too. He was only four the first time he disappeared and we found he'd slipped through the turnstiles at Maine Road one weekend, to see if he could watch Manchester City play. Hayley had frequent bouts of bronchitis and I worried for her future.

Later that year the Manchester vice squad decided to have a clean-up. I was arrested again and taken to Bootle Street police station. This time plain-clothes men from the vice squad started to question me. "Who's your ponce?" they asked. "I haven't got one." "You're a liar, Sheila. We know who it is. We've had our eyes on Calie Mottley for some time. He thinks he's clever but we'll catch him." They told me I was a fool not to name him and gave me a fortnight to reconsider. In exchange for a statement they offered me the run of Manchester for twelve months but I wouldn't give it to them, not yet. It was the time when they'd just introduced suspended sentences and I knew that, with three fines behind me, I was due for one of those rather than a prison sentence. Whenever I saw someone from the vice squad in the next few weeks I said that I was still thinking about it.

I'd told Calie about the arrest and the deal I'd been offered.

He was watching television with a bottle of beer in his hand and the kids were upstairs asleep. He wagged the bottle towards me and gave me a nasty look. "Well, sweetheart, if you turned me over, you know I'd kill you, don't you," he said. "It would mean six years for your man, and you wouldn't want to do that to me, would you?" I couldn't believe he'd get such a harsh sentence but he told me he'd already been to prison once for living off immoral earnings. It was the first I knew of his criminal record but I was beyond being shocked by anything Calie said or did.

Because I hadn't given the cops what they wanted they brought me to court. It was the old magistrates' court in Minshull Street and a drearier building you couldn't find. Everything was painted a mud-brown, even the toilet seats, and there were cold stone floors. As I'd expected, the magistrates gave me a three-month suspended sentence but I was a sitting target from then on. In fact I was trapped by my own lies. If I hadn't kept the Didsbury flat a secret from Calie, and hidden half my earnings, I could have continued to work from there and made enough money without going back to the Long Bar. Another possibility was to give up the game altogether, but by this time I had too much to lose. When I'd moved into Wythenshawe all I'd brought with me was one kitchen cabinet and a bed. Now I had fitted kitchen units, a three-piece suite, a very loud hi-fi and I could buy the kids clothes and toys. I simply wasn't ready to give all that up. So when Calie told me his friend's girl was working in Scotland, where the law appeared more relaxed, I decided I'd have a go up there.

He booked me into a hotel in Glasgow and put me on the train on Monday morning with all my bags. Anne moved into the Wythenshawe house to look after Neil and Hayley, and Janette was still at Margaret Barclay. I'd never been anywhere near Scotland in my life and all I had was the name of the hotel, the Dunsmoor. I was terrified that I'd arrive and no-one would have heard of the place but I needn't have worried. The taxi driver knew exactly where I was going. There were plenty of girls working out of the Dunsmoor, a seedy hotel at the bottom of Sauchiehall Street. The police had a very different attitude. They allocated a place for you to work and the hours you could be there. They'd pick you up once a week and keep you in the cells till three in the morning, then let you go without a charge, though just occasionally they'd have a crackdown and you'd be fined.

There were lots of girls there from Manchester, and the Glasgow prossies hated us. The punters were rougher, too, and they wanted a lot for their money. I didn't like being out on the streets again so I rented an apartment in Langside, south of the river. It was in one of those fearful old tenement buildings but it had massive rooms, fully furnished, and a splendid view across the city. I found I got a better type of client there, with one terrifying exception. I picked up a guy one evening in the city centre. He looked perfectly decent and he paid for a taxi to Langside without quibbling, but as soon as he got inside the flat he turned. "Right!" he said, putting a knife blade to my throat, "I'm just out after six years inside so don't mention money to me and I'm no wearing a rubber. Now get your clothes off." I escaped with some bad bruises and I was lucky that he was my first client of the night because when he'd finished, after about thirty seconds, he took all my money. It didn't amount to more than loose change, but I was scared as hell for a long time afterwards. I had a couple of stiff vodkas and went straight to the police. Word soon got round to the other girls and even the Scottish ones came up to see if I was OK and ask what he looked like.

I used to spend Monday to Friday in Glasgow and go home to Manchester for the weekend. One Friday when I returned, Anne told me that Calie had been sent to prison for failing to pay his maintenance. The police hadn't got him on the charge they wanted but it must have given them some satisfaction to have him inside for a short time. I made the most of the six weeks he was away. I cut my time in Glasgow down to three days and spent the other two days in my flat. During that time every penny I earned was my own. I bought a leather chesterfield and a new bedroom suite, had carpets laid right through the house, and got a convertible Triumph Herald. Of course Calie was very suspicious when he came out of prison and the first thing he wanted was my car, but I was having none of that.

The children got expensive new toys as well and squabbled over them as kids do. It was just Neil and Hayley at home and most of the time they got on very well. There were exactly three years between them in age and they could still sit playing with Lego together. It was before Neil became fascinated by model building and Airfix kits and paranoid about anybody coming near him in case they destroyed his delicate work. I found Neil easier to handle than Hayley who had a streak of defiance about her even when she was very small. She was a pretty thing, very dainty with an impish expression and those huge eyes with meltingly long eyelashes. But she was far darker then than she is now, and I worried about her being the odd one out. I had the feeling that perhaps if I had another baby by Calie, then it would be someone for her. The next pregnancy was the only one that I really planned, and I was pleased when the doctor told me I was carrying twin boys. I was perfectly healthy for the first six months and still travelling up and down to Glasgow each week when suddenly I was taken ill and found myself back in St Mary's. Apparently one of the twins had died and was putting the other in danger, so they kept me in hospital.

I was induced at eight months and Karl was born on 6th November 1967. He was a healthy baby and much lighter skinned than Hayley. As if to make up for the lack of flowers when Janette was born, I now found that thanks to my professional contacts I had more than enough. Every other day a new bouquet arrived from one of Karl's "uncles", and the nurses kept saying what a family I must have and how considerate they were. Some of my regular clients even came to the hospital to visit me.

Before I left hospital I was sterilised. It should have been a simple operation but I was apparently allergic to the muscle-relaxant they used and my heart stopped beating. I was on a respirator for twenty-seven hours and the police were sent round to my house with the news that I was dying. On the path outside they met Anne pushing Hayley in a pram with Neil and her boy Steven walking alongside. When she heard, she let go of the pram and it started running down the hill so the policemen had to chase after it. Later, Anne told me what a sight I was in the intensive-care ward, with tubes up my nose and wires everywhere. For a week or so she imagined herself having to look after a newborn baby and five others for the rest of her life, all on her own.

By the time I came out of hospital I'd lost a lot of weight. Winter was coming on and I didn't feel like going back to Scotland but I needed to buy things for Christmas so I started working from my flat. I was there early one evening when the telephone rang. It was one of my regulars telling me that the police had been following him around, which I couldn't understand because I'd been away so long. I was anxious but tried to put it at the back of my mind. Nothing else happened until February, but then they pounced. I was on my way to meet one of my clients in the Long Bar when a guy walked past me and all he said to me was "Are you free?" "No," I said, "I'm waiting for somebody." And that was it. I was nicked.

Now the bargaining started all over again. "Tell us who your ponce is and we'll let you off," and this time I knew the price of protecting Calie was a prison sentence. It was the hardest decision of my life and to this day I regret the choice I made.

Karl was four months old and the magistrate apologised for sending me to prison with such a young baby but said he had no choice because of my previous convictions and suspended sentence. He peered at me over the bench and I remember thinking how shiny he looked, as if he'd been scrubbed all over. He reminded me of a pork butcher. Although he kept trying to smile at me sympathetically, I was so angry, with Calie and with myself, that I just glared back.

I was sentenced to six months' imprisonment – three for the suspended sentence and three for this one, but they were to be served concurrently. I was less worried about the effect on Neil and Hayley than I was about Janette. The younger ones had Anne to look after them. Hayley and Karl were too young, I thought, to be really upset. They looked on Anne as a second mum, and Neil was best mates with her son Steven so he'd be fine. But I'd recently been visiting Janette at

Margaret Barclay every week, trying to get to know her properly before she came home for good. How could I now explain to her that I was disappearing for twelve weeks? As soon as I knew about the court appearance I'd warned her that I might have to go into hospital. Now I braced myself to phone the school and tell them this was happening.

Nothing had prepared me for the moment when the magistrate sent me downstairs to the container cells beneath the court. I looked at the rest of the girls in there – a pathetic load of scrubbers they were, and I thought "What on earth am I doing here?" I'd had my hair done specially for court and I was dressed smartly as usual, but now I was no better than the rest of them and about to go to prison. I couldn't believe it had happened to me. I think I must have felt I'd had so much rotten luck in other ways that I was somehow immunised against any more. But here I was, and perhaps anyone looking at us wouldn't have singled me out as someone special. I was just another tart who'd come unstuck. I listened to the others chatting and moaning about their sentences as if they were trips to the VD clinic, but I was overcome with a sickening sense of horror.

Chapter 7

PRISON PROPERTY

The prison coach drove along Upper Brook Street in Long-sight and I kept my head down in case anyone recognised me. The shrill chattering went on around me: "I hope Sheena's still in!" "If my chick's got anyone else, I'll kill her!" It was as if they couldn't wait to get to Risley to find out who was going with whom and I could have sworn I was going to a mixed prison. I felt disgusted.

There was one girl on the coach who seemed nicer than the rest. She was called Jean and this was her third time of going in. "Whatever you do," she advised,"if anyone touches you for a fag tell them no." I thought that sounded a bit mean but she repeated the warning and when I offered her a cigarette, she refused. "I'd love one but I'm not taking yours." She then took a small tobacco tin from her jacket pocket and started to roll a rather spidery cigarette. I'd never seen a woman do this before. She tried to show me how to do it, although I didn't really fancy learning this cheapskate skill. She also showed me how to split one match into four, which I thought was taking things a bit far. I didn't know that where I was going you had to make one box of matches last a week.

As soon as we drove in through the prison gates and into the reception area I felt as if I had stopped being human. I was now prison property. A burly female warder shoved me into a cubicle and ordered me to undress. I neatly folded up all my expensive clothes and put them in a tidy pile, but when I handed them over to the warder she screwed them up and bundled them into a plastic bag. She then flung a shapeless blue dress at me – size 14 – and told me to get into it before something nasty happened. I heard the girl in the next cubicle announce "I ain't wearing that! Give us one of them, miss, go on, with a belt round it. No, this is too long, this is. Giv'us a mini!" "It's your lucky day, Marilyn," came the reply, "just remember who's doing you a turn." There was silence for a few moments while the warder searched for another dress. "I don't know, Marilyn, what did you have to come back for, you're nothing but a nuisance!" You could tell the ones that had been there before and knew the ropes because they had the best cardigans, the best dresses, anything they wanted. But I was at the back of the queue stuck with a canvas sack for a dress.

I was still dolled up from the court appearance, with my hair lacquered into a glistening bouffant. The brute of a warder put her hands to it, looking for nits. I protested that my hair was perfectly clean and I'd been to the hairdresser only the day before. "Ooh look at Lady Bountiful!" she mocked. "We'll have to do something with all this, won't we?" and she wrenched her fingers through my hair. She had a face that looked as if someone had jumped on it and I was ready to do the same.

The next indignity was the detailing of personal possessions. I had about eighteen cigarettes left in a packet and £120 which I'd brought in from the night before last. I presumed I could buy more cigarettes with my money but another warder took great pleasure in telling me that I couldn't touch my belongings again until the day I walked free. Any money I needed inside would have to be earned. I'd been systematically stripped of everything that made me a person. I simply couldn't understand how only last night I'd been tucking up Karl and trying to get Hayley into bed and now here I was, banged up, for trying to look after my family. I knew I was no angel but I couldn't understand why I was being treated like a villain.

"Miss can I go with Susie?" "Oh, miss, can I share with her?" the pleas went on, but I was put into a cell on my own. I was shaking as they locked me in. I looked at the door and thought "I can't go home to my kids" and then it hit me. Someone nearby was having a leaving party and the place sounded more like a zoo than a prison. I think I must have cried all night, because there was banging on the wall and shouts to belt up. Next day I had to wait to see the governor. My eyes were red and sore and my hair was a shaggy mess. She looked at my notes and said, "You've got children haven't you? And one of them's handicapped? Who's looking after her?" But I wasn't going to tell her because I didn't want Janette's school to know where I was.

They put me on scrubbing the yellow brick road. It was a corridor that winds and winds its way through the prison and never ends. Work started in the morning and we were still scrubbing at four in the afternoon. I was hard at it the first day when one of the screws stopped me. "It's Sheila Finch, isn't it?" she said, using my maiden name. I looked at her hard and remembered her from school. She told me to let her know if there was anything I needed and she'd try and get it for me. I'd have been all right at Risley. People say it's bad but it was the Hilton compared to where I was going next.

I was at the remand centre for eight days before being transferred to Holloway. During that time I had one visit from Calie and he only came because he wanted to find out where I'd left my money. I couldn't believe his brass. I'd made elaborate arrangements with Anne and I wasn't going to tell him about them, so he went away fuming, unsatisfied and grumbling about me! On my last night there one of the girls in the cell next to mine tried to kill herself. She was about to be parted from her lover and had gnawed at her wrists.

On the way to London we travelled in a green bus with tinted windows. The screws sat at the front with our property in plastic bags. They were a decent lot, and let us have our cigarettes. Jean and I sat together again and she continued my prison education. "Aren't there a lot of lesbians?" I whispered. She said, "If you think this is bad, wait till you get to Holloway!"

The stories she told me about Holloway made me shudder, but they were fairy tales compared to what I found. It was the drabbest, most cold-hearted place I'd ever seen. When we'd arrived and they'd unloaded us from the bus, they took some pride in showing us the grave of Ruth Ellis, the last woman to be hanged in England, making it seem like a grisly sightseeing trip.

After stripping in a cubicle we were sent into a massive shower and hosed down together. It made me feel as though I was taking part in one of those films about concentration camps, but there was no play-acting about the harshness of the water or the degradation of all those naked shivering women. From the day you go into Holloway, all privacy has gone. You're not even a name, just a number. I became 8045697 and I was on B Wing. They put me to work in the jam factory and it was awful. On my second day I was bending over to lift up a crate of jam when I felt a hand up my skirt, a woman's hand, and it made me feel soiled. I suppose I should have been used to sexual approaches from strangers, but I'd somehow grown up with the idea that sex between women was nauseating and I felt completely repelled by it.

Our cells were disgusting. The wooden stand for the wash-basin was thick with grease and I was afraid to touch it. Slopping out was dreadful. The screws would open up the whole landing, not three or four cells at a time like at Risley, and women would often collide in the rush for the lavatories. One morning I saw a new girl on the landing, gingerly carrying her bowl at arm's length. The warder we all hated most was on duty that day, her face set in a twisted grin, and she calmly stuck out her foot as the girl went past. Of course there was a crash and shouting and the new girl was told to stay behind and clear up the filthy mess she'd made. I thought that she was just throwing her weight around as usual, but there was more to it than that. When we next saw the girl she was in a right state and that evening everyone on B Wing was saying that the screw had forced her to have sex in her cell. I was quivering with fright after that, because I was sure it would be my turn next.

There was no doubt that the younger and prettier prisoners seemed at greatest risk from some sort of assault. I decided that the only way I might survive prison life was to make myself look as sloppy and unattractive as possible so that none of the dykes wanted to touch me. During recreation, when the prisoners danced and snogged in pairs with the screws watching, I clung to my seat at the edge of the room and refused to move. I stopped using make-up and only washed my hair every couple of weeks. But there's no accounting for people's taste. I then started getting love letters from a prisoner called Ivy, followed by messages from her jealous girlfriend about how she'd kill me if I so much as shared a bar of prison soap with Ivy.

But I was saved from any experience like that by an altogether different ordeal. I hadn't been in Holloway long when I started to haemorrhage. It was about two in the morning and I put my finger on the bell and kept it there. Other prisoners shouted at me to shut up but I yelled out that my cell was full of blood and that got them ringing their bells as well. By the time the screws came it was gone four o'clock and my sheets were soaked through. They sent for two male warders who carried me over to the hospital wing and from there I was transferred to a hospital about ten minutes from the prison. It would have been a relief to be out, except that everyone knew I was from Holloway. There was another prisoner in my ward who'd committed infanticide and then tried to strangle herself with a curtain. She had a guard in her cubicle who kept watch on me at the same time. But I was only kept in for a few days. I think I'd had the haemorrhage because of all the heavy lifting in the jam factory, so soon after I'd been sterilised. The doctors were convinced I was four months pregnant and having a miscarriage, and after giving me a D and C they sent me back to the prison hospital wing.

There was one nice warder there called Mrs Kramer. She stood by my bed one day and said, "I know no-one's happy in here unless they're out of their minds, but you look really miserable. What's up?" So I told her how frightened I was of some of the women, and how I was dreading going back to B Wing where I was sure I'd be attacked by that brutal warder. She seemed sympathetic to that and a few days later told me she'd been reading my notes and seen that I'd done eighteen months of my nurse's training. She asked me if I'd like to stay in the hospital wing and help the nursing staff. I jumped at the chance, even when she told me I'd be sleeping in an eight-bedded dormitory with a number of women who'd committed very serious offences. "You can't make me go there! I won't sleep a wink with all those murderesses!" I said, but she told me I'd be safer there than in a room of my own. These women were in Holloway for observation, while psychiatric reports were drawn up, and most were on heavy medication. She said she could do with some extra help keeping an eye on them and with my nursing experience I'd be very useful. And I think I ended up doing a valuable job. I stopped one woman from slashing her wrists, and I got another one, who hadn't spoken a word about her crime, to tell me all about it. Not that it made enjoyable listening. She described how she'd lost her temper with her toddler and hurled his high-chair to the ground, smashing his head.

One of the eight beds was occupied by the most beautiful African girl I'd ever seen. Everyone knew her as Gloria, but she didn't respond to anything. For at least two weeks she'd been lying in bed with her arms folded across her chest and her eyes fixed on the ceiling. Apparently she was from a wealthy family and her husband was a surgeon. She'd lost her first baby at full term and it had obviously unhinged her because she'd gone out one day and snatched someone else's child. Now she was in Holloway on remand, while the authorities wrote psychiatric reports. I thought someone should write psychiatric reports on the authorities, because this girl had been put in a bed between two women who'd had perfectly healthy children of their own but had killed them. Although Gloria didn't speak to anyone, it didn't mean she couldn't hear or notice what was going on. I used to wonder what on earth went through her mind when she heard those two creatures bragging about murdering their babies. It certainly couldn't have done her much good.

Although I couldn't get any reaction from Gloria, I felt very protective towards her. I noticed one day that she was wearing a silk dressing-gown which was fastened with a tie at the front, and I felt suddenly worried in case she tried to kill herself. Mrs Kramer assured me someone would have checked to make sure the tie was properly attached to the gown, but I still felt uneasy. When I'd finished following her on her rounds, I went back to the dormitory and saw at once that something was badly wrong. Gloria's beautiful dark face had turned purple, and her eyes were bulging. She was still lying down, but

threshing around and holding her hands to her sides. The silk
tie was wound tightly round her neck. I started to pull at the
scarf, to no effect, and pummelled her chest while screaming
out for an ambulance. Soon a couple of nurses came tearing
in, we got the scarf off and she was whipped away to a
resuscitation unit. Mrs Kramer told me later that she'd
recovered and a few days afterwards I heard that Gloria had
left the prison hospital and had been sent to a psychiatric
hospital.

By now, I was being trusted with as much personal freedom
as is possible inside a prison. Obviously they couldn't leave me
with a pair of scissors or a scalpel, but I was given some
responsibility for patient care, such as assisting at medication,
changing dressings and so on. It was great to have a useful job
to do, though I can't say I took to the patients particularly.
Even when they were laid low, most of the prisoners were a
really tough bunch.

Occasionally though I came across someone who seemed to
be inside through no particular fault of her own, or whose
petty crime could surely have been punished in less devastat-
ing ways. I had no quarrel with the law for sending me to
prison but what I think confused me, as well as some of the
less hardened cases, was why being inside had to be made so
horrible. Jean used to say that we were locked up as punishment, which was fair enough, not locked up so that we could
then be punished.

My release date was 25th June, nine weeks and five days
from the day I went to prison. I hadn't seen any of my kids
in that time because I wanted them to think I was in hospital. Whenever I wrote to them it was on ordinary paper,
not the prison issue, and when Neil asked to visit me,
Anne made some excuse about me being too ill. Calie never
came to see me either – he said he was none too fond of
prisons – and I can't say I minded. Watching the other
girls who came back on the wing from a visit, I could see
how upset it made them. I was still very anxious about
Janette but I knew dad was visiting her regularly.

The day before my release I was allowed to have my own
clothes back and wash and iron them. Then there was a pep

talk from the governor, which in my case was totally unnecessary because I had absolutely no intention of ever coming back. The punishment of being inside, even just for three months, was quite enough for me. That night some of the other girls gave me a party and I ended up having to comfort a couple who seemed sorry to see me go. I was woken at six the next morning and when I stepped into my clothes I felt they didn't belong to me any more because I'd grown so thin. I looked at my hair, with all the black roots showing, and it was like seeing a complete stranger in the mirror.

I got back the £120 they'd taken off me when I first arrived at Risley, and took a taxi straight to Euston. They'd given me a travel warrant for the train to Manchester, and I'd been in two minds about whether to use it. I decided it was daft to spend my own money when I could travel free, but I regretted that decision when it was my turn in the queue for tickets! I handed over the warrant and cringed as I saw the big letters saying Holloway Prison. I was convinced everyone behind me was looking at them. I felt then that it was like being branded and I'd have to carry the marks on me for the rest of my life. All the way home on the train I thought that everyone could see where I'd been and I wondered if I'd ever recover from the shame of it.

Chapter 8

BEGINNING AGAIN

It was thrilling to get out at Manchester Piccadilly but I was that jittery about going home I could almost have caught the next train back to London. I'd never been away from home for such a long period. Sometimes in Holloway I couldn't even recall what the children looked like. Now I was expecting all sorts of things to be different and couldn't believe that everything seemed the same, from the colour of the buses to the same old posters on the hoardings. Although I was bursting to get home, I decided to catch a bus to gradually soak up the delight of being back, and confirm with myself my plans for beginning again.

The first thing I was going to do was give up the flat. All I had to do was drive round, pick up my bits and pieces, and return the key. Then I'd have to organise my social security, get us all a larger house from the council, and then bring Janette home. In this reverie, I found myself walking up to my own front door and my heart jumped when I realised I was about to see three of my kids. Anne was virtually waiting for me with a wonderful cup of tea and took me into the lounge, which the three children had completely taken over. As I stood there in the doorway, Neil glanced up from the floor with a smile, said, "Hi, mum", and carried on looking at his comic. Karl was sprawled out asleep on his back on the sofa and Hayley took absolutely no notice of me at all. I'd been expecting to be suffocated in loving hugs. I thought I'd burst with disappointment but standing there I made myself realise that it was daft to expect anything else, and that I needn't have worried about them because Anne had obviously done a brilliant job.

We sat chatting and she told me that Calie hadn't bothered

to come round and see the children all the time I'd been away. Then a few days before I was due home he'd turned up in the morning when they were all out and pinched some money Anne had put aside in a drawer. It was the savings she had ready for a home of her own. I didn't know what to say to that. It was one thing having him mess up my own life, but I couldn't bear the thought of him ruining things for a good friend like Anne. I promised I'd give her whatever money I could, but now I was off the game there wasn't going to be much to spare. I told her she could stay with us for as long as she wanted and then I set about making my own plans for a fresh start. First of all I pestered the council till they found me another house which was suitable for a handicapped child. They could see I meant business and pretty soon we moved to a new place in Parrs Wood Road, in Didsbury. It would have been perfect if it hadn't been such a busy main road, but I thought we'd learn to live with that. The only thing I couldn't get used to was that Karl had got into the habit of being put to bed by Neil. Every day now, after his tea, it was "Nee Nee, go bed," and Neil would heave him upstairs, tuck him up, and stay with him until he was asleep. It was wonderful being back with my family, but this bedtime ritual was a living reminder to me of what I'd done to us all.

Anne found a place of her own before long, on the other side of Manchester, and we were all sorry to see her go, especially Neil. But I was too busy to miss her. I was arranging the next step in our lives, which was to bring Janette home. It finally happened late on one Friday afternoon when she was driven home in the school ambulance. We'd arranged a party and had a big blue and white streamer slung across the front of the house saying "Welcome home Janette. This time it's for good!" She was six years old. One of the ambulance drivers wheeled her in with a lapful of toys, while the other one brought in cases, carrier bags and baskets full of all the possessions she'd accumulated over the years. The other three children were dressed up in their best clothes, excited about seeing their older sister and anxious to get their hands on the crisps, coke and chocolate cakes laid out in the kitchen. But after the first rush of enthusiasm the atmosphere became a bit quiet and strained. Janette sat in her chair in bewilderment. She hadn't had much to do with her sister and brothers and I think she was overwhelmed by them. Neil wanted to play with all her toys – he'd never seen so many in his life – but she wouldn't part with any of them. Hayley wouldn't go near her, and Janette tried to baby Karl who was just old enough to object.

I knew there were things I'd have to sort out before long, but I didn't want to spoil her homecoming so I tried to divert everyone's attention by taking Janette to see her new bed-room. I'd spent hours making it look nice, but after surveying it with a critical eye she complained that she didn't like the pattern on the curtains. I was convinced that if she'd actually had arms and hands, she'd have been sitting there resting them on her hips. I meekly promised to find her some curtains she liked.

For all of us it was a period of readjustment. Janette had to get used to being part of a family, coping full-time with younger brothers and a sister, and they had to make room for a very bossy older sister who needed a lot of attention. And I had to learn to lead the life of a reformed character, an ordinary housewife with three small children and a demanding handicapped daughter. I can't pretend I didn't miss my flat and the companionship of the Long Bar. I missed dressing up in my glad rags to escort one of my regulars to a dinner dance or a show in town, and I missed the income. But the day I left Holloway I vowed that I'd never risk going back, and besides, at first I had too much of a battle on my hands to get bored.

The city council wanted to send Janette to a school for the mentally handicapped but I wasn't having any of that. One of the reasons she'd become unhappy at Margaret Barclay was that she was so much more intelligent than the other children and found them stupid and irritating. So I looked around for an alternative and found a Roman Catholic school called the Hollies where the head-teacher said she'd be happy to have Janette, so long as the education authority agreed to provide a lift and ramps for getting her up and down stairs. Well that seemed a perfect solution, but unfortunately the education authority refused to give the money, insisting she should go to the school of their choice. It was stalemate, but I wasn't going to give in. I kept Janette off school and waited for them to take me to court.

Sure enough the education welfare officer came along and told me I was breaking the law by keeping Janette away from school. That wasn't all I was breaking, either, because the tension at home was getting worse with Janette being there all the time. The welfare officer told me that I could be fined and Janette could be taken away from me. I was getting very anxious at all this but about a fortnight before I was due to appear in court I was called in to see Manchester's education officer, Mrs Nora Regan. We hit it off right away. She told me she had a granddaughter she thought the world of, who had suffered some slight brain damage which affected the limbs on one side. She asked me to go and look at her granddaughter's school and see what I thought of it. "If it's for mentally handicapped children, I'm not going," I said, but she assured me it was for the physically handicapped.

The school was called the Lancastrian. It was a big red-brick building which had once been a school for the blind and it was on the Cavendish Road next to the Withington Hospital. I knew at once that it was the right place for Janette. The walls were covered in paintings the children had done and there was a happy atmosphere. I arranged for her to start the very next day and, when I fetched her home that evening, she was full of it. She babbled about it to all of us, from when she got home, during tea, bath-time and into bed, telling us everything she'd done, what the teacher had said and giving us the low-down on all the other children in her class. That was Janette's schooling sorted out but the next thing I had to see to was making life easier at home. Janette was getting too heavy to carry and we needed a lift to get her up and down from her bedroom. The housing department said that structurally it was impossible to fit one and instead offered me a house in Wythenshawe. I didn't really want to go back there because of some of its associations with my wicked ways, but I was tempted by the house itself, which had a big garden and a huge hallway.

Moving house also gave me the chance to shake off Calie.

He had stayed with us in Didsbury for several nights a week and he'd been in and out of work, selling encyclopedias and doing a milk round. But he had the unfortunate habit of paying his takings into the bookies and he never held a job down for long. At the time of the latest move he was working for Corona, selling bottles of pop.

I made sure that we moved on a Saturday because it was his busiest day. But he wasn't that easy to get rid of. Somehow he found out we were in Wythenshawe and on the Monday after we moved he went round every school in the area till he found Neil. The first thing I knew about it was when I got a call from Neil's headmaster. He said there was a coloured gentleman in his office who said he was Neil's father. I tried to explain by saying that he was Neil's stepfather, and then he called Neil out of class and let them speak to each other. That was the end of my secret and it had terrible repercussions. I was standing at the cooker in my new kitchen that evening when Calie appeared in the doorway. His face was like thunder and he just walked over and kicked me the length of the room into the back garden. After that there was no getting rid of him.

A few weeks later I decided to call my dad. I'd been feeling guilty about cutting him off from Janette. While she was living away from home he'd been able to see her regularly but since she'd been back with me he'd lost touch and I knew how unhappy that must have made him. The last thing I wanted was for grandfather and granddaughter to drift apart, so I swallowed my pride and rang to ask him round. He sounded pleased on the phone and, of course, there wasn't a word about my black boyfriend. He said he'd been missing Janette and he'd come and see us the next day. I made a special tea for him and put all four children in their best clothes, but as soon as he arrived on the doorstep I knew it was a mistake. He'd brought presents for Janette and Neil, but nothing for the others and all the time he was there he was cuddling the oldest two, yet he didn't once touch Hayley or Karl. We ended up having words. He told me he knew everything I'd done since I'd left Gordon Avenue and he couldn't understand any of it. He also accused me of not visiting my mother. When I told him I'd been to see her at Prestwich nearly every week he didn't believe me. So I described the ward she was in and how she couldn't even recognise anyone any longer, not even me. That quietened him down for a while. But by now it was me who was angry. I told him not to bother coming back until he could treat all his grandchildren in the same way.

I bent over backwards to make sure that, wherever possible, the kids were all treated just the same as each other. Of course Janette needed a lot more of my time and attention, but if they got a treat she got a treat, and if they got a slap when they were naughty, so did she. I was always having to break up fights between the four of them. Janette never got used to sharing her toys and she'd be furious when Neil took them off and started taking them apart to see how they worked. He never knew how to put them back together again and ended up with a black eye on several occasions – Janette's revenge on these occasions was still a violent head-butt. The younger children resented the time I spent with her. In fact they found her a bloody nuisance. Consequently, there was hardly a moment when one or other of them wasn't whining "Mu-um, Neil's touching my things!" "Mu-um, Hayley's got my radio!" And then: "Mum, Janette won't let me play with the jigsaw!" "Mum, Janette's not letting me look at her books!"

Karl was the only one allowed to play with Janette's toys. She still loved mothering him and he'd become used to it by this time and enjoyed being spoiled. She always had a hold over the younger ones and could usually make them do whatever she liked. I found that Neil had disappeared one day and it gave me the fright of my life because the front door was open and traffic was roaring past outside. I screamed out for him, and Janette calmly announced that she'd just given him some money to buy some crisps from the shop across the road. I tore out of the house and found him standing on the pavement waiting for a gap in the traffic. I was yelling so hard that I'm surprised he didn't run away from me but I scooped him up and back into the house. There were other times when I caught Neil doing something stupid or naughty and I knew Janette had put him up to it. I suppose she was getting him to do the things she desperately wanted to be able to do for herself. Later she used to manipulate Hayley in the same way.

The Lancastrian opened up a new life for Janette and taught her all sorts of skills I'd never dreamed she'd have. She hadn't been there long when I had a call from her teacher asking me if I could spare an afternoon to come over. There was nothing to worry about, she said, but she had something to show me. When I arrived I was directed to the school's hydrotherapy pool, where I saw Janette sitting on the edge at the far end. "Hi, mum!" she shouted, and before I had time to blink she'd disappeared over the side into the water. I panicked and was just asking myself whether or not I should dive in when the school physiotherapist touched my elbow and told me not to be alarmed. A moment later, Janette bobbed up like a cork, lay on her back in the water and started propelling herself with her little flippers towards me across the pool. I couldn't believe my eyes. The grin on her face when she reached me was broader than the Cheshire Cat's.

Later she took it into her head to learn to sew, but even the school thought that was impossible. She'd have to hold the needle in her mouth and they were worried she'd swallow it. But again, Janette's determination won the day. They fixed a square of material onto a wooden frame and I was brought in to watch as she painstakingly pushed the needle through, put her face under the material and pulled it out the other side.

One of her new school-friends was a boy called John Newton who lived near us in Wythenshawe and wore calipers. They visited each other's homes and we used to tease them about being sweethearts. I remember one afternoon in the summer when John arrived with his mother to find Janette in the paddling pool in our back garden. She was just at an age to be self-conscious and it had taken a lot of persuading on my part to get her into the pool in her swimming costume. When she saw John standing there in the garden she went blood-red with embarrassment and I reckoned she would have preferred to drown in the few inches of water rather than have him looking at her. But then John's mother told him to take off his clothes and join her! For years after if any of us wanted to make Janette blush we'd remind her of how she sat in the pool alongside John Newton in his underpants.

Janette wanted to be part of anything that was going on.

She never let her handicap get in the way. So I found myself going to the local Brownie pack and saying that my daughter had no arms and no legs but she'd like to join. I don't think they knew how to refuse and along she went. It was good for both of us. It got her away from the television in the evening, and it gave me a bit of a break. It was quite a long way to the Brownies' fairy glen but I bought a sturdy double-seated pushchair. I'd put Janette on one side, Hayley on the other, and have Karl sitting on a kind of tray on the top, while Neil walked alongside. These were happy times. Money was short because all I had to live on was social security payments and maintenance from Terry, but the children were contented and on the whole they got on well together. The younger ones were sometimes jealous of Janette and annoyed that her needs had to be put first, but if I couldn't give them the attention they wanted they always had each other to play with. Calie spent time with us when it suited him and the younger ones were always overjoyed to see him. Even Janette learned to tolerate him and, sucker that I was, I still welcomed him with open arms until we had one row too many and I ended up with concussion and another set of bruises.

We'd been in the Wythenshawe house a few months and the council were just getting round to installing a lift, when the gas board came to convert the street to North Sea gas. They disturbed a brook and within three months there was fungus on every wall and so much water downstairs that we had to wear wellingtons in the hall. They found us a temporary home in Hulme, a maisonette in one of the new high-rises. Today it's considered one of the worst blocks of flats in Manchester but we were among the first to move in and we loved it.

Janette was coming up for eight years old and it was here that she got her first electric wheelchair. It was paid for by the Lady Hoare Appeal which had been set up several years before to help thalidomide children. They'd given various amounts of money for Janette's clothing and if there was any equipment that could help her they'd always pay. But she never appreciated anything as much as this chair. For the first time she could go off on her own without having to ask someone to take her. There were four big crescents where we lived, joined by walkways and ramps, and from that moment Janette was always out, whizzing from one to another like a kid on its first bike. She also discovered the delight of chasing her smaller brothers and sister. Karl was three and terrified of Janette's car, but I wasn't going to spoil her fun by telling her not to go after him. It was more independence and she relished it.

I was grateful to the Appeal for the help they gave. But as a single parent with two half-caste children, the do-gooders who administered the Fund always made me feel a bit of an outcast, not quite as worthy as the other parents. Once a welfare officer arranged a holiday for us all in north Wales. It was quite unusual for the Fund to pay for me and the other kids as well as Janette but this was an exception, and I made the most of it by persuading them to let me take Anne and her two boys as well. We were driven to Rhyl in a mini-bus and the six children never stopped singing all the way. But they stopped pretty smartly once we arrived. We'd been posted to an old RAF camp in the middle of nowhere and it was completely deserted apart from ourselves and a grumpy couple who were in charge. Our billets may have been home sweet home for wartime airmen but sleeping on straw mattresses in Nissen huts didn't seem quite like being on holiday! I kicked up an almighty fuss and we were grudgingly allowed into the so-called luxury bungalow. Spartan would have been a better description. Impossible as it was to imagine, we were assured the place would soon be teeming with healthy holidaymakers but that it was now off-season. That obviously accounted for the rain. We spent the week being ferried in and out of Rhyl by our mini-bus driver, a right patsy who burped all the time, to the kids' delight. I know the Appeal welfare officer had no control over the weather but she couldn't have chosen a wetter time to send us to the seaside. We tried to amuse ourselves among the haberdashers' and ironmongers' shops in the town before returning to lights out at eight o'clock in a freezing cold bungalow.

When we got back to the warmth and comfort of Manchester I described the conditions to the Appeal Fund and they were so upset by the news that they promptly gave us a free holiday at Butlins!

I got my revenge on that horrible welfare worker a few months later by chasing her out of my house. She'd always seemed patronising, and when I went to prison she'd made it her business to find out where I was. I had my suspicions she might have been the one who told dad about Holloway and I was certainly worried in case she discussed my past with the other thalidomide parents. Now I decided to cut my links with her blessed Fund. "Stuff you lot!" I thought, "I'll get along on my own."

Not that this was easy. Those extras for Janette made all the difference to my household budget, and without them I found myself struggling to keep us clothed and fed. I remember walking to the shops in the rain one day with my shoes worn right through and Calie coming to me and saying he'd pay for some new shoes if only I'd sleep with him. I refused. I'd really had enough of him by then. The fearful memory of his blows helped me stick to my resolve. On the whole I managed pretty well with the three young ones and Janette, and some people were very kind. The driver who took Janette to and from school each day used to pick up my shopping list in the morning and return with a parcel and sometimes a bag of coal in the afternoon.

By the time Janette was eight years old the campaign for compensation for thalidomide victims was gaining momentum. Hardly a week went by without some mention in the newspapers. One group of parents had already received a settlement from Distillers back in 1968 but there was another, larger group now demanding compensation. The main legal argument was about how much each child was entitled to, taking into account his or her life expectancy, how much he might earn and so on. After a High Court decision, it was settled that a totally limbless child could receive £106,000, but under the terms of a previous decision a forty per cent deduction had to be made, which apparently resulted in a lump sum payment for such a child of £9,600. It seemed that the more the lawyers tried to help the parents the worse things became. The situation was complicated because of course not all the children could be treated as identical. There were various degrees of disability, and it wasn't always easy to prove that thalidomide was the cause. Parents who didn't seem to have a very strong case were under pressure to accept any offer, while those with cast-iron cases were inclined to fight on for a fairer deal. There were sixty-two families who had accepted the earlier settlement from 1968, but largely through my own ignorance, Janette and I were in the bulk of the remaining three hundred and seventy cases who were determined to get a more honest result.

Calie was going on at me all this time to see if I was entitled to something but I resisted it because I knew he'd figure that he was entitled to something too! He wasn't even Janette's dad, though when the mood was on him he made a decent enough father. Then one day a new welfare worker turned up on my doorstep, very well-spoken and in a tweed suit. She told me that I only had a short time left to make a claim for Janette. I wasn't sure I could prove that it was the drug which did the damage but she took down copious details of my pregnancy and everything that had happened. After filling in all the forms I thought nothing much more about it till a letter arrived asking me to take Janette back to Alder Hey for an examination. The poor child had to stand naked while she was measured and photographed and she put up a loud fight till I told her it was the only way we'd ever get any money from Distillers, the company who'd manufactured the drug that had made her the way she was. This medical assessment turned out to be quite important though at the time I'd rather have been at home with Janette watching *Blue Peter*.

Several months after this, late in 1971, I was summonsed to a big meeting at the Adelphi Hotel in Liverpool. Kimber Bull, the firm of solicitors acting for most of the parents in the thalidomide case, claimed they had important news about an award from Distillers and meetings like this were taking place all over the country. When I arrived the room was already packed with families and the mood was electric. None of us had any idea what to expect, but our hopes were high and we were buoyed up by all the sympathy generated by press reports of the terrible damage to our children.

I was sitting halfway down the conference room, next to

Ruby Astbury, a mother from Chester with a son called Freddy who was three years older than Janette. There were children there as well and they were all fidgeting and the grown-ups were chatting so that it seemed more like going to a Christmas pantomime. Then at last one of the lawyers got to his feet. Immediately there was silence. You could almost hear us holding our breath as he read from a prepared statement. He indicated that they had now got the best possible deal we could expect from Distillers and that we should all sign and accept it on the spot. He told us that Distillers had offered to put £3.25 million into a charitable trust from which the afflicted children could draw as they needed it. If the lawyer expected cheers of delight he was a disappointed man. Not only was it a pathetic sum but it would only be paid by Distillers over ten years, generally reducing its helpfulness to parents struggling with the emotional and physical costs of disability. He then went on to tell us that our children had been divided up into an X list and a Y list. On the X list were children whose disability was unquestionably the result of the drug, and on the Y list were those whose case was uncertain. In other words, Distillers were still quibbling over a number of cases where, for example, parents had no evidence of having taken Distaval under prescription. No-one could believe it. We were asked to line up and come to the platform at the front of the hall where we were to give our names and learn which list we were on, X or Y. Later we'd be told what this meant in terms of a financial settlement. The real problem was that our lawyers were urging us to settle without knowing exactly what it was we were agreeing to in terms of compensation.

As people returned to their seats after learning about their assessment you could tell immediately from their faces where they belonged. Some walked back looking relieved but a bit embarrassed. Others had expressions of sheer disbelief which quickly turned to anger. The slow shuffle forward to the platform seemed to take hours and I found myself walking like a robot, empty of any feeling except curiosity. Which list would Janette Mottley be on – would it be X or Y? Suddenly I was at the front of the queue and the man at the desk was

Mum and Dad on Blackpool Prom just before they adopted me in 1941.

The day of my first Communion when I was eight. *Below right,* on holiday with Mum and Dad at Middleton Towers Holiday Camp, where I won the Prettiest Princess competition.

Coronation Day 1953 and the street party in Stanhope Street, next to Gordon Avenue. I'm the farthest back on the right wearing a white hat.

This was taken at my last school Christmas Party, when I fourteen and a half years old.

Janette and me.

Left, Janette just after she was fitted with her plastic arms.

Janette at Marple Children's Hospital where she learnt to walk on her "rockers." *Above*, dancing to her favourite Beatles song "Love Me Do."

Janette growing up. *Above*, with her friend Kevin at Alder Hey and *below*, making headlines on her tenth birthday.

Colour comes to limbless girl's life

HEARTBREAK TURNS TO HAPPINESS

By JACK SHEPHERD

HEARTBREAK turned to happiness this weekend for one of Britain's severely handicapped thalidomide children — thanks to the News of the World.

Bright and cheerful Janette Mottley, who was born 10 years ago without arms and legs, has never used a colour television set for her birthday tomorrow. But she seemed doomed to

disappointment until her mother, 30-year-old Mrs Sheila Mottley, of Charles Barry Crescent, Hulme, Manchester, turned to us for help.

She explained that she was planning to buy the set out of the £1,500 damages which she agreed to accept in November last year from Distillers (Biochemicals) Ltd., the distributors of the drug.

But she has now discovered that the £340 which also included £340 a year for Janette out of a £1,250,000 trust fund, has lapsed.

Shock

That shock news was given to her on Friday when she approached her bank manager for an advance on the cash which she would receive soon after last Christmas.

The manager decided to

check on the delay with the thalidomide parents' solicitors in London and was told that the offer had been withdrawn.

"I felt really shattered," said Mrs Mottley. "Janette had set her heart on getting a colour TV — she wants one more than anything else in the world. I could run all the way out to I ran to a phone box and rang the News of the World."

As a result Janette will get her colour TV after all. Because as soon as they heard the story, the parents' solicitor immediately made arrangements to advance Mrs Mottley enough money to cover the purchase of a set.

They explained yesterday that the damages offer was made on condition that all

the parents of 374 thalidomide children accepted. But five refused and in the Appeal Court earlier this month they were given the right to sue the company.

"So the irate Distillers laid down could not be excepted," he said, "and the offer has lapsed automatically as I think they are likely to make a new offer but these negotiations have not yet started and it may be the middle of next month before they get under way.

Grateful

A letter is being sent out to all parents this week-end asking them to sit tight until then. But I certainly feel there will be a settlement before the end of the year."

Mrs Mottley, who was told three months before Janette's birth that her child would be deformed, now has two sons and another daughter and makes ends meet by working as a nurse at the hospital where Janette was born.

"I had never heard of

thalidomide children at the time," she recalled. "I thought I was to blame for it at first.

"In November it looked as though all our financial struggles would soon be over and that we could get more money soon after Christmas.

But now it seems as though we shall have to start waiting all over again.

"But we are all very grateful to the News of the World for helping to make Janette's birthday wish come true."

At that moment, Janette, back home from school where she is said to be one of the brightest pupils, was pushed into the room in her wheelchair.

"Hello," she said when we were introduced. "I'm going to have a colour television for my birthday on Monday."

Happy birthday after all for Mrs. Mottley and her daughter Janette.

READER GIVES AID TO FOI... IN F...

VITAL research into the baffling illness agoraphobia (morbid fear of public places) due to be abandoned because of lack of funds, will now go ahead, thanks to the News of the World.

Two weeks ago we reported that questionnaires completed by 1,500 women sufferers were lying because there ... £200 available ... them analysed.

Now a News ... reader, ... personal ... offer of ... of ...

When night porter went to her room

E of the duties of the night porter at a seaside hotel was to make routine s round the rooms. But what happ- n Room 26 was no part of his job.

... room at the sea-front hotel in Folkestone. 54-year-old Mrs Christina Peterson, own from Sweden for her son's

FOR FOOT SUFFERERS

LIGHTWEIGHT SPRING/
SUMMER SHOE. STYLE W1773.

Chi-Chi

CHI-CHI, Lon... alone with ... A zoo sp... and ... Chi...

Me and Kelli-Anne in September 1986,
when she was just five days old.

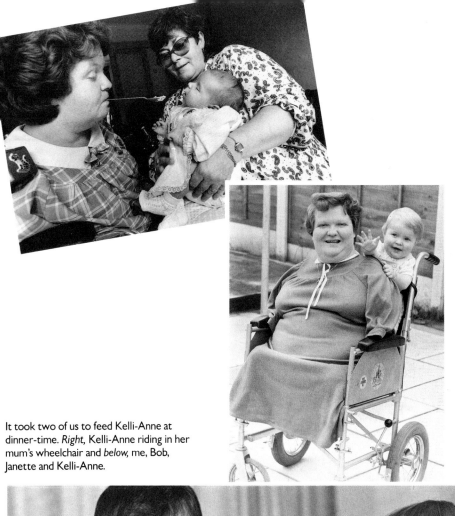

It took two of us to feed Kelli-Anne at dinner-time. *Right,* Kelli-Anne riding in her mum's wheelchair and *below,* me, Bob, Janette and Kelli-Anne.

Nana! Here I am in 1987 surrounded by my grandchildren. I'm holding Regan and Neil's daughter Janine, with his son Dale and Kelli-Anne at my feet. *Above,* my latest grandson, Karl's first child, Kyle, born in March 1991.

Below, Regan and Kelli-Anne, Christmas 1990, and me at my surprise 50th birthday party, arranged by Janette, Bob and Kelli-Anne in June 1991.

looking through the names. "Mottley, initial J," he read out. "You're on the X list. Distillers recognises liability."

Chapter 9

THE SETTLEMENT

'The Distillers offer was worth £5,000 for each child on the X list. They also increased the £3.25 million trust sum to £5 million. At that time they assumed there would be three hundred and forty-two who would benefit and individual sums would vary according to an assessment of the child's disability. This would be determined at yet another physical examination at Alder Hey. We heard this news at a second meeting in Liverpool, and afterwards I walked to the car-park with Ruby Astbury in total silence. The Distillers' offer now meant an average of £17,500 for each child. Her Freddy was on the X list like Janette but I think we'd both made our minds up that the fight for justice for our children was only just beginning. It was good to have Ruby as a colleague in arms. She had the same tough outlook as me, but more importantly she kept me in touch with what was going on. The two biggest parents' groups were in London and Liverpool. I think I must have been the only person in Manchester with the thalidomide fight on my hands and it was a pretty lonely business.

Ruby and I decided to raise money for the campaign against Distillers and their paltry offer. I felt I'd sat back long enough and let other people got on with it and now it was my turn to do something. I went all round Manchester asking people to boycott Distillers' products. I also approached the students at the polytechnic because I thought they'd be the best people to organise a demonstration. We made huge banners and stood outside some of the large supermarkets which stocked Distillers brands. I know we didn't do a damn thing to Distillers colossal profits, but even these puny efforts to strike back made us feel better, and it was a useful introduction to manipulating publicity for the campaign.

Up to this time, I'd been led to understand that all the parents had to have the same firm of solicitors. But someone told me that this was nonsense and that we could choose for ourselves so I contacted the firm in Manchester that had always looked after our family's affairs. From then on, Mr Hoolohan of Briggs, Whitworth and Weir dealt with every offer that was made to me and I thought he did a far better job of it than those southerners at Kimber Bull. He came with me and Janette for her second assessment. She had to strip to be photographed and examined by Professor Smithells and after this examination I was told that we'd be notified about the final offer.

My bank manager, Mr Gardner of the Royal Bank of Scotland, also turned up trumps. Even before the final settlement from Distillers was approved by the High Court, he loaned me various sums of money in advance. As well as the compensation due to Janette, I had been promised £5,000 in damages. In fact the original proposal was £2,500 for me and the same for Terry. I had to battle to get both halves, but my case was made easier because apart from not having anything to do with her, Terry had twice been inside for non-payment of my maintenance. One of the things I was determined to buy out of my money was a colour television set for Janette's tenth birthday in April 1972. Mr Gardner had agreed to lend me the money but when I went to collect it he greeted me with a long face and said, "I'm sorry to disappoint you, Mrs Mottley, but I've just learned that Distillers have withdrawn their offer." Apparently six parents had refused the company's terms and one of them, David Mason, had appealed against the offer and won in the Court of Appeal. Although that put the kibosh on Distillers' puny settlement it meant that we'd all have to start again. I was glad that Distillers would be taken back to court, and it was one in the eye for the government and the health department, but my immediate thought was about breaking my promise to Janette. But all this exposure to wily drug companies, solicitors and the like, was quite an education for me and I was beginning to learn a few tricks of my own. I contacted the *News of the World*, who'd carried stories about thalidomide children, and told them what had happened.

They offered to talk to the bank for me in exchange for a story. Subsequently the bank advanced me a year's rental on a television for Janette and the newspaper sent a reporter round to take a photograph of us. So Janette got her birthday present, and the newspaper got a story about how "heartbreak turned to happiness thanks to the *News of the World*", with a picture of me and Janette right across the front page.

This certainly wasn't the last bit of craftiness on my part when it came to protecting Janette's interests. I couldn't believe how Distillers could be so arrogant and dismissive of the children's rights, but they always seemed to behave as though the parents were the guilty ones for taking their wretched drug in the first place. I'm pretty certain they felt that they had the government nobs behind them, and that if they just stuck it out then we'd all get fed up and go away. Even I used to think that my misdemeanours seemed pretty thin compared with what Distillers had done.

By the summer of that year we were on the move again. The Hulme maisonette wasn't that suitable for Janette and the council found us a smashing house in Radlett Walk at Long-sight, which they fitted with ramps and a lift. Janette always insisted on having a bedroom upstairs, and for the first time I didn't have to carry her up at night. We were all very happy in that house, though for me it was a period spoiled by Calie's behaviour. He was still walking in and out of my life at irregular intervals. Occasionally I compared notes with his wife Julie and we agreed that he must be having an affair with someone else now because there were times when neither of us could account for his whereabouts. But bastard that he was, I wasn't able to free myself from him altogether. He was the same attractive guy, full of bullshit but with a smile that could crack tougher hearts than mine. And the kids were always glad to see him, especially Neil for whom he was always dad. I spent a lot of time chatting to people about getting rid of him once and for all but when the time came, it wasn't my doing.

It was coming up to the Christmas of 1973 when Calie got a call from Barbados to say his father was seriously ill. I hadn't spoken to my own dad since his visit to Wythenshawe but all of a sudden Calie took it into his head to take Janette to see her grandad. What he was really after was his return fare to the Caribbean, and somehow he managed to get it. I was shocked that he'd sponged so ruthlessly from the one person he knew who would be delighted to have him out of Manchester, even for just a few weeks. I was so grateful to dad, though, for giving him the money that I had another go at having him round for tea. This time he was sweet to all the children and there were no recriminations. We talked about everything just like old times when I was living at home. A few weeks later, by the time Calie was back from Barbados, dad and I were fast friends. He helped babysit sometimes and we took to visiting mum together at Prestwich. Her condition had deteriorated and in January 1974 she was seriously ill.

She had a series of blackouts and every time she came out of them, she seemed to be more vacant. I can't remember how many times dad and I were called out because the nurses thought that she was dying. Each time we arrived to find that they'd just managed to save her life but I honestly wondered sometimes if it had been the right thing to do. She looked as wasted and helpless as a baby rabbit, her eyes wild and puzzled, unable to account for her pain and misery. Dad and I could hardly bear it and we'd drive home sobbing all the way. The only difference was that I was crying for dad, while he was mourning what had been his wife. This final phase lasted about three weeks but dad was so upset by it all I asked the staff not to call us out again until it was all over.

Several days later I arrived home late one night. I'd given the babysitter a heap of fifty-pence pieces for the gas meter and as it was still loaded with them I settled down for the night on the settee in the lounge. I woke towards morning feeling very chilly, and saw that the gas had run out. It was 5.15 a.m. and I decided to make some tea and stay up. At eight o'clock dad rang to say that he'd heard from the hospital that mum had died. I gasped. "Was that at quarter past five," I asked him. "Your mother died at five-fifteen," he said. "How did you know that?" I suppose it was coincidence, but it was blooming funny that a full meter ran out at the same time as mum breathed her last.

When they did a post-mortem they found out that the cause of death was a brain tumour. Perhaps that had been the main cause of the trouble all along, not Alzheimer's. If they had only had the brain scanners that they have nowadays they might have been able to operate and cure her.

The business with the gas meter wasn't the only weird thing that happened about that time. Janette had a lot of electrical equipment which she operated by sucking or blowing on a tube which set off a control system called Possum. A few weeks after mum's death it all started going haywire. We'd be woken in the middle of the night by the sound of the video and the radio, the lift would be going up and down, doors would be opening and the lights switched on. We had a cupboard with sliding doors where I kept my brushes and cleaning things. One night I'd been up switching everything off and for some reason I opened this cupboard and there she was. My mother. It's strange but I wasn't at all surprised, or frightened. Suddenly it dawned on me that she was the one playing around with the equipment and I was furious. I was about to give her a piece of my mind but when I looked for her, she'd gone.

After that it went quiet for three or four nights but then it happened again. I stood at the top of the stairs and yelled, "If you don't stop this bloody racket, mum, I'm going to get the priest in to see to you." That only made things worse and the next night she started banging pans about in the kitchen. The house was becoming like a fairground so I decided I'd have to carry out my threat. I called the priest in and he went round the house blessing each room. That should have been the end of it, and for us it was. But a few weeks later the woman next door came and knocked at my door. "Sheila," she said, "don't think I'm being daft when I ask you this, but have you ever seen a ghost?" "No," I lied. "Why do you ask?" The poor thing looked terrified. "Well I've got one! It tried to smother me last night by putting a pillow over my face!"

After the dead had stopped bothering me, it was the turn of the living. Calie had never exactly been one for settling down, but after he came back he seemed more restless than ever. On his sickbed Calie's father had made all sorts of promises and Calie wanted me to get Janette's compensation sorted out so that we could all go and live in Barbados as a family. I wasn't really tempted. Janette would never have got the same medical attention and I didn't want to throw in my lot with Calie. I was very suspicious about his interest in the thalidomide case. He was always asking about the money from Distillers and harassing me to buy tickets for Barbados. Then in the summer we heard that his father was dying and he wanted to go out straightaway. This was the chance dad had been waiting for. When Calie asked him for money a second time, dad agreed but only on condition that it was for a one-way ticket. He was buying him off, I suppose, and Calie didn't put up any resistance.

Hayley wasn't really affected by her dad's going but Karl fretted and Neil was even more miserable. We didn't hear from Calie for about six weeks and I must admit it wasn't the happiest period of my life either. I missed the good times, and in a way I even missed the rows. Although I'd fought to get rid of Calie, I'd still say he was the only man I've ever truly loved. Mind you, what I learned after a few months of his absence should have killed any feelings I ever had for him. A friend from the band told me that Calie had sent for Julie and his other kids and they'd gone out to live with him. I had to come to terms with the fact that Calie had intended this all along. He probably wanted Janette's compensation so that he could hand it straight to Julie and his legitimate family. I was even told that after I'd seen him off from Manchester Piccadilly, he'd got off the train at the next stop to pick up his eldest daughter and they'd travelled together to the airport and then to Barbados.

I was lonely without him, but it was Distillers who suffered most from his absence! I busied myself with the fight to keep Distillers and their behaviour in the news. Most of the thalidomide families in the north-west came from around Liverpool and I was the only one campaigning in Manchester. I got to know all the reporters from the *Manchester Evening News* and one way and another I think we kept them going with stories. However, the crucial newspaper was *The Sunday Times*. I was more of a *Sunday Express* reader myself and simply thought of *The Sunday Times*, if at all, as a paper for rich people. But for years they had been investigating the story and finally, in September 1972, they ran a three-page story which got the ball rolling. Because of the amazing stranglehold which Distillers' own lawyers had on the case, the paper wasn't able to tell the whole truth of the story. To get round this, the editors decided to concentrate on the moral justice of it all rather than the legal fight. The headline which did it was "Our Thalidomide Children: A Cause for National Shame" and the report went on to say that the behaviour of the government, the lawyers and of Distillers shamed British society.

After huge amounts of press and also parliamentary activity, thanks to the MP Jack Ashley, and a rebellion among Distillers' shareholders, a final settlement had been approved by the High Court in July 1973. This was worth £20 million in total, and was made up of £6 million to compensate the 340 outstanding cases, and annual payments of £2 million to a charitable trust for the next seven years. Following her assessment, Janette was offered £32,990, and that really did seem as much as we could hope for. In fact it sounded like a fortune, until I sat down to think what it was needed for and how it was supposed to make up for the loss of arms and legs. Anyway, after the offer it was just a question of keeping up the pressure on Distillers and waiting. But I was sitting at home one night watching the evening news on television when there was an announcement that the Inland Revenue were going to tax us on the income from the charitable trust set up by Distillers. The next thing I knew the phone was ringing and Ruby Astbury, calling Harold Wilson's government every name under the sun, was saying that Freddy was going on hunger strike in protest. I told Janette what Freddy was planning to do and she looked very interested indeed. Then the doorbell rang and there were our friends from the *Daily Mirror* asking for my reaction. Janette wanted to talk to the reporters for herself and she told them that she was going on hunger strike too. I was grinning with pride at her – eleven years old and holding her first press conference!

The next day I was driving through Manchester and I saw

newspaper placards saying "Thalidomide girl goes on hunger strike!" Lots of people thought I was dreadful allowing my child to starve herself but Janette had become determined to make a protest. I made sure she stoked up with hot soup and drank plenty of tea. Besides, she and Freddy were both over-weight and a quick diet wouldn't do either of them any harm. Needless to say, all the national newspapers got hold of the story and next thing we knew Janette had a phone call from Jack Ashley promising his support but begging her to give up the strike. He had campaigned brilliantly and I'd have done anything for him, but Janette wasn't so easily persuaded. We had groups of newspapermen practically living with us during this feverish time. Speeches were made in the House of Commons and within days the Prime Minister, Harold Wilson, intervened, calling for emergency talks with his Chancellor, Denis Healey. Then it went quiet for a bit, which made it even harder for Freddy and Janette to cope. Then victory came, with Harold Wilson announcing that the government would top up the charitable trust with £5 million to offset the income tax. We celebrated with a huge meal afterwards, which of course made Janette feel even worse than when she wasn't eating!

Janette and Freddy went back to eating big meals again but nothing could stop the protest in London which Ruby and I helped to organise. Hundreds of thalidomide parents were to march to Downing Street on 30th October 1974. Janette and Freddy, who were enjoying the limelight, wanted to come too but not with each other. In many ways they looked alike – chubby cheeked with curly hair – but Freddy was an arrogant fifteen-year-old who never said please or thank you and Janette disliked him intensely. It was odd because Freddy was one of the first thalidomide babies to be born, and Janette was one of the last. But Ruby and I got along. I think some people found her a bit of a pain in the neck but I was always grateful for the way she'd befriended me when most of the other parents seemed to ignore me. So our two families, supported by loads of students from the north-west, travelled down to London by train and the atmosphere was more like a beer outing than a genuine protest. We had our banners stored in the luggage racks and we sang songs like "We Shall Over-come". Janette thoroughly enjoyed herself. I've always been terrified of London but that day I didn't mind the crowds and the impersonality of the place. In fact I looked up at Big Ben and the grand Houses of Parliament and thought, "We're as good as anyone in there and we're going to make them take notice of our children!"

The trouble was, there weren't many of our children there for them to see. Quite a few were in residential homes like the Chailey Heritage Craft School and Hospital in Sussex, hidden away from public view, and I knew that others were kept at home away from the glare of strangers in the street. I could understand parents wanting to protect them from cruel re-marks but I couldn't help feeling that some of them were ashamed of their children and that's why they had left them behind. There's no doubt that people in the street can be horrible towards nature's victims on occasions. I never knew which was worse for Janette, people shrinking back in amaze-ment or pretending that she wasn't there. The trouble is that no-one ever teaches their children how to respond or behave towards people with disabilities and so they just pick up their parents' or friends' prejudices. But I wasn't too worried about Janette in London. She always answered back and was quite capable of outstaring anyone who seemed too curious.

She was now turning into a very self-possessed young lady. I'd stopped calling her a child on the day I got another phone call from the Lancastrian. This time it wasn't to request my presence at the swimming pool but to pass on some news. Janette had insisted I be informed that she'd started her periods. It was a moment she'd been anticipating, almost hysterically, for months and I'd begun to worry she'd never start. But the teacher told me Janette was thrilled to bits. She was the only pupil, she said, who was delighted rather than terrified by the event.

In Manchester, Janette was really something of a celebrity. I think everyone admired her determination to live life to the full. She would have a go at everything from discos and girl guide outings to the young people's disabled Olympics, where she won a gold medal for the electro-slalom in her wheelchair, and a silver medal for target bowls, which she played with her mouth. Whenever there was a charity event for children, she'd be invited. When the Variety Club of Great Britain bought a mini-bus for Manchester kids, they wanted a photograph of Janette inside. When the city's taxi drivers held their annual outing for disadvantaged children, Janette was in the leading cab. She went to Lourdes on her thirteenth birthday on an outing sponsored by the Church of the Holy Name, and she had a holiday each year organised by the charitable trust. It was wonderful for her and no less than she deserved but it was hard on her sister and brothers. They were sick of me saying, "No you can't go because that's just for Janette." And I hated it when photographers would push one of them aside saying, "Out of the picture, kiddy, it's your sister we want." If I had my time again I'd have insisted that the younger kids were at least allowed to appear in the photos with Janette, because it caused a rift between the kids too deep to heal. Even if I had managed not to spoil or indulge her, I couldn't have prevented other people doing it. When we waved her off on one of those outings I'd turn to the other three and the envy on their faces made me want to weep. And I had no answer for Neil the day he said, bitterly, "I wish I had no arms or legs then maybe I'd get some of the things Janette has!"

Unfortunately Janette didn't make it easier for them. She'd boast about all the treats. "I'm going to Blackpool tomorrow and you're not coming!" "I bet you'd like to go to Lourdes, Neil, well you can't!" And she'd come back full of her adventures, stuffed with ice-cream and sweets and loaded with more presents. She was no better at sharing her possessions. When she got a new television, thanks to the charitable trust, she insisted that it was in her bedroom so that the others couldn't watch it. And she kicked up a fuss if I tried spending any of her clothing allowance on the others. I'm afraid that this behaviour over the years made Neil grow to hate her. It's painful to think of one child actually hating another but I think that's how Neil felt about Janette. He certainly refused to do anything for her, though sometimes he did help by taking her out, possibly because she always had money to spend.

Karl was the one who got on with her best. However tall he grew, he was always her baby brother and they were very alike in temperament. Whatever they set out to do, they put heart and soul into it, and they always wanted to come out top. Neil and Hayley were hopeless at school-work but Karl and Janette did well. It was Janette Karl turned to when he had problems with his homework and they'd sit together doing fractions or spelling while the other kids fooled around. But I always tried to praise each of my children for the things they were good at. Neil had a real talent for drawing and making models. Hayley could have become a model of another sort, she was that pretty, and she was also very good at athletics. At one time the runner Sharon Collier offered to coach her in the 800 metres but, as with everything else, she soon lost interest and put her running to other uses instead.

The Distillers' settlement made Janette a wealthy young woman. In August 1975, when she was thirteen, I was called to the High Court in London with Mr Hoolohan to see a judge in chambers. It was a massive building with marble floors and decorated ceilings and pictures in alcoves. I was completely overwhelmed by the size of it. We went into an antechamber and there was the judge in his gown and wig and Mr Hoolohan sat in front of him with a bloke from Distillers, and I sat behind them. They were all terribly polite to each other and there was a whole load of legal twaddle before Mr Hoolohan said that I was the child's mother and had accepted the offer on her behalf. The judge called me "my dear" and asked me to come down to the front. He looked a bit worn and frayed at the edges but he had a kind smile and he talked to me about what a shock it must have been when Janette was born and what a strain it must have put on the family. "You're going to have to think very seriously," he said. "You've got to decide at what age your daughter should come into her money." He reminded me that it was a considerable sum but that it would have to last Janette's lifetime and then he asked me if I'd decided. "Oh yes, I'd decided before I left home," I said. "I don't think she ought to have the money till she's twenty-five." He asked me to give my reasons and I said I knew only too well how many heartless people there were in this world, who'd try and get what they could out of you. By the time she was twenty-five Janette would have had the opportunity to learn the difference between friend and con-artist.

He seemed to think this was a sensible decision. The money had to be put into a trust and I appointed Mr Hoolohan and Mr Yarker of the bank trustees. Many of the thalidomide families who'd had early settlements had lost a lot of their money by investing unwisely and I was determined not to let the same thing happen to Janette's income.

"Well, have I got it?" asked Janette when I returned home. £33,000 was as good as a million to a thirteen-year-old and I think she expected me to hand her a stack of crisp fivers and turn her into a fairy princess on the spot. I told her about the trust, that she wouldn't really get any income from it for the first year and that the judge had agreed it was best for her to be twenty-five before she had control. And I explained that there was money from the trust to pay for holidays and that we'd go out and buy some new clothes for her the very next day.

But the one thing you can't buy is affection. I tried to get Janette and Hayley close by asking Hayley to do personal things for her, like helping her undress and taking her to the bathroom and for a while it seemed to be working. At one time there was a lot of whispering between them and although I'm not keen on secrets I tolerated it because it was the start of a relationship. Janette even began buying Hayley some clothes. Hayley was a very pretty child, slim and big-eyed and Janette would make her parade up and down in skintight jeans or pretty skirts as if she was on a catwalk. "Not like that! Put your hands on your hips, Hayley," she'd say. "Go on, stick your chest out, that's better!" Looking back on it I suppose she was using her sister a bit like a walking Barbie Doll, or perhaps she was getting her to act out the Janette she could never be, just as when she was smaller she'd get Neil to do the naughty things she couldn't do. Poor Hayley, though, couldn't under-stand it when Janette suddenly tired of this game and her source of clothes dried up altogether. She tried to blackmail

Janette by threatening to pinch clothes if Janette wouldn't give them to her, knowing the effect that would have on me. It was a threat she carried out, but I wasn't aware till much later.

I had the brainwave of asking the Lady Hoare Appeal to give Hayley some money for being Janette's carer but it wasn't a success. After just three days I walked into an unholy row between them. "I don't want your frigging money!" Hayley was shouting. "I might be black but slave labour's been abolished!" I couldn't help laughing. It reminded me of all the times I'd seen the kids creep past Janette's bedroom door on all fours rather than catch her attention and have her call out "Fetch me a drink, Karl, I'm thirsty", "I need my pencil sharpened, Neil!" or "Hayley, come here and fasten my buttons. Quick!"

You have to be a Henry Kissinger to handle a family like mine. Life on the streets was much easier and there were many times when I looked back with nostalgia. Distillers may have been goaded and shamed into making me comfortable financially but increasingly the other areas of my life seemed a complete mess.

Chapter 10

ON THE REBOUND

Once the fight with Distillers was over I decided to concentrate on enjoying myself. I was still in my thirties and the kids were becoming older and more independent. I could see my life stretching ahead of me but I couldn't see what the hell I was going to do with it. I was missing Calie like anything and to drown out the pain I took to drinking heavily and going out on the razzle, coming home in the early hours with the milkman. Sandra, a friend of the family, was staying with us at the time and she was happy to look after the kids for cigarettes and lager.

There's quite a lot of that year, 1975, that I simply don't remember and much of it I'd prefer to forget. The episode with Ken for instance. He was a black lorry driver I met at a party given by my next-door neighbours. He was an unstoppable show-off and always cackling at jokes – usually his own. He said he was a true cockney, as if it licensed him to play the fool all the time, and though he was exhausting to be with he was a terrific tonic. He made for me the moment I walked into the party and before I knew where I was it was morning and there was his face on the pillow and his shoes at the foot of the bed. The kids had been missing their dad and they warmed to Ken right away, probably because his humour was about their level. He started taking Karl on his haulage trips, which did the lad a lot of good because it meant personal attention and a man to talk to. Ken swept me off my feet for a while with his over-the-top declarations of love, and with all that vodka or gin inside me I was easily swept! He drove me down to Lambeth in south London to meet his brothers and sisters and they welcomed me with big hearts and open arms.

It wasn't long before he'd proposed and I found myself up at the register office, showered in confetti and surrounded by laughing black faces. We had a brilliant reception with a steel band, though not the Royals, and hundreds of glasses of bubbly. But the bubbles soon burst. It was only a matter of weeks before Ken gave up his job saying he wanted to spend more time with me. Then he started stopping out all night and would only come in to change his clothes. Once he brought home a rather shy young woman who wore lashings of bangles and bright lipstick. He introduced her as his cousin and I fussed around making her sandwiches and tea. It was only when Ken had taken her off for a drink that evening that I grasped she was probably his fancy piece. If I'd had my wits about me I would have realised that I'd been taken down this path before, but my mind was so clouded with confusion that I'd have not even noticed the bus to Belle Vue if it had stopped and asked me the time.

Janette's rehabilitation officer, Jane, arrived one day shortly after this. "Have you got something to drink, Sheila?" she asked. "Why? Have you had a row with your boyfriend or something?" "No," she said, "but you're going to need a stiffie when you hear what I've got to tell you!" Jane said that when Ken had applied for social security the DHSS had checked his records and discovered that he was already married and his wife and three children were living in London. So now I was married to a bigamist! If that didn't bake the biscuit I don't know what did. I felt completely stuffed. With all the other things that had happened to me I couldn't understand how the good Lord had the nerve to throw this at me as well. But then I burst out laughing. I was relieved, really, because I knew I'd made a mistake with Ken and this was the way out. I could have wallpapered the lounge with all the "I told you so's" from dad but that was a small price to pay for my independence.

I'd promised Jane that I wouldn't say anything to Ken until the authorities had taken action. I think she was worried that he might turn nasty. I waited for a week but then I couldn't contain myself any longer. All that man was coming home for was to have a bath and a shave and go out again. I didn't want to give him any warning before I called the police because he'd be out of the house and off in my car before I'd hung up, so I decided to watch for his car. The next time he turned up I dashed into the kitchen at the back of the house and made my phone call. When I'd done it I stood listening to the taps running upstairs, thinking, "You cocky bastard! I'm going to get you!" "Where are you off to, then?" I asked him, leaning against the bathroom door. "Out," was the reply, "and it's none of your business!" So I told him he could pack his bags and clear off because I didn't want to see him again. "You ain't giving me the old heave-ho," he crowed, "this house is as much mine as yours." "That's just where you're wrong, you sneaky great toad!" I screamed at him, adding that I was going to call the police, and knowing of course that they were on their way. I had to hand it to him, though. He just carried on shaving and eyeing himself up, saying smugly that the police wouldn't want to know because we were married. At that I couldn't hold myself back any longer. "That's where you're wrong, chuck!" I said, pouncing on him from across the bathroom so that he cut his face with his razor. "Bloody married, are we?" I screeched. "What about your wife in London then and her three kids? Bloody well married! You can clear off now!" In fact it was me that cleared off downstairs then, in case he walloped me.

He wasn't in any hurry because he didn't have anywhere to go. His "cousin" Belle was living with another fellow and only wanted him part-time. But I told him, "I don't give a monkey's where you go, as long as it's out of this house!" and when the cops arrived I put them in the picture. Unfortunately they wanted proof so I gave them Jane's number. They said that was no good because it was Friday and the social services department would be closed. Marvellous. Then they went upstairs to see Ken and I could hear them asking him to leave peaceably rather than wait for any trouble. There was an almighty scuffle and one of the coppers got cut. I don't think it was intentional but of course Ken was still standing in the bathroom with his razor in his hand. Well, that was that. They had him downstairs and into the back of their van in a blue flash. They said they'd keep him in custody till Monday and then they'd check out the bigamy. They also said I should take out an injunction to stop him bothering me. They were nice lads and I thought about offering them a cup of tea. It all seemed more like the council's pest-control unit arriving to deal with a large rat than taking away someone whom I'd married only a few weeks ago.

On Monday I got a phone call from Belle saying Ken had been given bail but he needed £300 surety. As far as she was concerned, to me she was just his cousin, but she had the neck to ask me if I was going down to the police station to get him out. "Tell you what, darling," I said. "It's you he sleeps with, so you go down and you get him out. Personally, I wouldn't bother. I'd wait for his wife and three kids to come and fetch him home to London," and with that I slammed down the phone.

That was the end of it. I saw him a couple of times after that driving a taxi, and each time he pulled over and greeted me as if we'd been old school-friends. I can smile about it now but at the time it was the final straw that drove me over the edge. I started going out, clubbing it, putting away the booze like nobody's business. There were the odd flirtations with good-looking con artists from all round Manchester. One guy in particular, Sammy, was very persistent, but he had a wife and grown-up kids and I wanted nothing to do with him. He was away in Barbados when I went to a big dance at the West Indian Centre. The good old Royals were playing and I was enjoying myself on the dance floor when suddenly I noticed I was being surrounded by a ring of youths, tightening in on me in a really menacing way. They turned out to be Sammy's kids, and I think I'd have been scarred for life if someone hadn't tugged me out of the circle and hauled me through the club onto the street.

It was George, the straight-laced drummer from the band, and goodness was I glad to see him. I thought this is the second time someone from the Royals has plucked me out of an unsavoury situation. He stood me outside the hall and told me I was to go home at once and that when the dance was finished he'd be over to check that everything was OK. Sure enough he called in that night at Radlett Walk and he gave me a few home-truths. He said it was terrible to watch a nice girl like me turning into a drunken slut and if I didn't sort myself out soon I'd be beyond help and all my kids would be taken into care. If dad had been saying these things I'd probably have told him to stop interfering in my life. As it was, I sat meekly with George in the kitchen, drinking coffee, and listening to some very painful truths about myself.

It was wonderful, in a way, to have someone showing some genuine interest in me for my own sake. I seemed to have become nothing more than a servant for the kids to boss around or a soft touch for all the deadbeats in Manchester. George was a respectable sort and I had a lot of regard for him. I knew he was right and when he left I gave him a hug of thanks, which seemed to embarrass him, but it felt as though I'd been to confession and I felt tons better. George became a regular visitor after that, partly to see me and partly, I think, to see Janette. He'd known her since she was a tot and always had a soft spot for her. Gradually he became part of our lives. He straightened me out, pushed out various spongers and hangers-on I'd attracted since the compensation arrived, and even stopped me drinking.

By the time George had finished cleaning up my life I didn't have any friends left. One by one he froze them out, saying that only when I got some real, genuine friends would he be nice to them. Once he came in to find me and a girlfriend at the kitchen table with a bottle of vodka between us. He picked her up in the kitchen chair, put it down outside in the garden and slammed the door. That night, when George was out with the band, her husband came round and heaved a brick through the window, but that was the last I saw of her. I don't think I was sorry. I realised that she was the same as the others. It was always my booze they were drinking and my cigarettes they smoked.

Dad fell for George much quicker than I did. He thought he was just the sort of gentleman I should have settled down with. George was adorable in his way, and I grew very fond of him, but it wasn't the passionate love that had existed between me and Calie. He moved in with us, though he kept his own flat, and he was as steady as a rock. He'd had the same job as a welder for the past nineteen years and he never took time off, not even sick leave. The only rows we ever had were over the children. The boys weren't much trouble at first. Neil was a good bantam-weight boxer and spent most of his time at the club, and Karl was totally involved in the Young West Indians' cricket team, but Hayley was beginning to go wild. She'd never say where she was going, she'd stay out late and there seemed to be no way of controlling her. She'd been caught pinching from local shops but didn't show the slightest shame at what she'd done.

In his teens, Neil looked as if he might go the same way and I was beside myself with worry. It was as if one minute he'd been playing cowboys and Indians and the next he was truanting and staying out all night. Since Calie had gone I seemed to have lost all influence over him. It was as if there was a huge gulf between us. I think the only thing that kept him on the rails was his ambition to join the army. He'd been drawing and dreaming soldiers since he was a young boy and he knew he had to keep the record clean if he wanted to become one. George blamed me for being too soft on the lot of them and there were many occasions when he wanted to put the strap to them. They were forever griping about him to me, and he was going on at me about them and I felt like a punchbag in the middle.

Janette was the only one who didn't cause me any trouble as a young teenager, although she embarrassed me rotten sometimes because she was a brazen flirt. From a very young age she seemed to understand any dodgy joke or sexual innuendo from adults. She had plenty of friends of both sexes and a very active social life. They'd all go out in a group and sometimes a girlfriend would stay overnight and they'd be giggling into the small hours. She was now working for her CSEs and her school reports were always excellent. Janette has tremendous powers of concentration and usually pulls off whatever she sets out to achieve.

From the £6 million invested in the charitable trust for all thalidomide children, Janette got an annual income of several thousand pounds. It was to pay for carers, clothes, holidays and any special item like an electric wheelchair or a car. Receipts had to be produced and every penny accounted for.

In fact the trust was worse than the DHSS in its fussiness over the children's money. But although I hated the bookkeeping side of it, I was always glad that the accounts were there for anyone to look at and check. Each year there was money left over and Janette was beginning to accumulate a tidy sum. So when the trust suggested the children put some of their money into bricks and mortar, it seemed a good idea. Janette was enthusiastic about having her own house and I thought I'd put some of my own savings into it, but the trust wouldn't hear of that because everything had to be for Janette and nobody else. George kept his views to himself but dad was dead against such a move. "Janette will leave one day," he said, "and then what will you do about the house?" As I couldn't envisage a day when Janette wouldn't need me I started house-hunting.

In Trafford we found the perfect house. A beautiful big semi on the corner of Wordsworth Road, with four bedrooms and a garage for two cars! The owner wanted £12,500 for a cash sale and we couldn't hand the money over fast enough. We'd never lived anywhere like it. It was the kind of place where you washed the car every Sunday in the driveway before going off to play golf. Dad used to get an extra kick from visiting us there, and I swear that George grew even more respectable. We hadn't even got enough furniture to fill a quarter of the house. Then an auntie of mine died, and continuing my run of good luck she left me a bit of money so Janette and I went halves on some new carpets and chairs and bedroom fittings. I wanted to pay half the rates, but again the trust wouldn't let me, so I just paid my share of the gas, electricity and telephone. I was well and truly Mrs Suburbia now.

George was nothing if not a creature of habit. With his moustache and heavy square glasses you'd have taken him for a bank manager if he hadn't been black. We had got into a snug routine of television suppers and early nights. I washed up and tidied while he mowed the lawn and if we felt really daring we'd go down to the pub for half a pint of shandy. I didn't even go out with the Royals when they were playing together. George could sense that I was getting a bit restless though, and he encouraged me to finish my nurse's training and go back to work. It was typically sweet of him to think that I should go out to work for my sake, unlike the leader of the band who had sent me out to work for his sake! I found that the experience with my sick mum had given me a special feel for psychiatric nursing and I relished the companionship of a ward and the sense of having some of my own money again. Poor George. Without realising it, his kind thoughtfulness had given me a taste of freedom and I came to realise that playing happy families wasn't really my scene. I adored George and couldn't bear to hurt him but in my heart I knew this cosy life couldn't go on. He calmed me down and sorted out many of my problems but I have to admit that living with George, for all its relaxation and comfort, was ever so boring.

When Janette was sixteen she left the Lancastrian with three CSEs and was offered a place at Hereward College of Further Education in Coventry. I could tell she was itching to be away from home and lead an independent teenage life, and I was really glad she had this opportunity. The college was for the physically handicapped and she was down for a City and Guilds course in community care and a few O levels.

However, before she went, there was something I felt I had to get straight with her. I'd always been frightened that she'd eventually hear about my past, and I wanted to be the one to explain it to her. In a way I was pushed into this by dad. We'd had one of our periodic rows and I'd told him not to come to Wordsworth Road any more. I was exhausted with hearing about all the mistakes I'd made in my life and I needed a break from him. He retaliated by leaving a note for Janette stuck on the fridge with a toy magnet, saying he had important things to tell her. I immediately guessed what kind of things these might be. That evening, after I'd managed to get Karl and Hayley into bed, I asked Janette and Neil to sit down for a chat. We were in Janette's bedroom and they were larking about but I made them realise this was serious. Then without any flannel I told them about the life I'd led with Calie, how I'd been a prostitute and had gone to Holloway. What I couldn't tell them was that I'd had a choice – either go to prison or shop Calie. Keeping this a secret turned out to be a terrible mistake but at the time I felt it had been my decision and my life and there was a limit to what I could share. When

I'd finished talking, I looked up at them. There was a long silence. On Janette's face there was a look of horror and disgust. She didn't cry and she didn't speak but I knew she was devastated. Neil, on the other hand, leant forward and put his arms round me. "It's all right, mum," he said with a sniff, "it doesn't bother me."

Neil has never been ashamed of that part of my life. Perhaps he associates it with the good things he had from it, such as the treats and the toys. But Janette is quicker to make moral judgements and I think it shattered the illusions she'd had as a child of a glamorous mummy who could do no wrong. From then on she wouldn't talk to me for a long time and there was a terrible atmosphere in the house. We managed to patch things up before she left in the ambulance for college, but it was a relief when she'd gone. I felt sad, of course, and the house felt strange but the other kids were openly delighted. We all went up to Blackpool for the day and for the first time I realised how hampered we'd been by Janette's disability. Whenever we'd gone there before, I'd stay with Janette in her wheelchair on the front while Hayley and the boys played on the sand. But of course Janette soon got bored and I'd have to drag them away. Now that we were on our own we could lark about as we liked. All four of us took off our shoes and ran barefoot along the shore, kicking, splashing and laughing our heads off like a bunch of loonies.

I'm afraid it was one of the last times we were so happy together. Neil was spending more and more time away from home and Hayley was turning into one hell of a problem. I used to dread that late-night knock on the door and the sight of the patrol car outside. "What's she done this time?" I'd ask without waiting for an introduction. By the time Hayley was thirteen she'd been expelled from her convent for bashing up the nuns, and become a regular visitor at the police station. After several appearances in the juvenile court, the magistrates pronounced her beyond my care and control. She was sent to a family group home but because she threatened to kill the younger children there they booted her out. This time she was put in a bigger home, like the one I'd been sent to as a teenager. Far from being ashamed of it, she seemed rather proud. It certainly wasn't much of a punishment because half the kids inside did frequent runners, Hayley included. While she was there I read in the paper that two girls had knocked a woman down in the street, kicked her and snatched her purse and her jewellery. I don't know why but something told me that my daughter was behind this. I rang the home straight-away and asked the care assistants to confront her. Sure enough the silly bitch had a newspaper cutting about the incident on her table and a pawn ticket for the jewellery was found under her mattress. By now even George's patience was wearing thin. I knew I was a failure but reprimands from George and dad only drove me to my wit's end. My GP sent me to a psychiatrist but I only saw her twice. All I needed was someone to tell me I had to say "No" to my kids instead of letting them get away with blue murder, and that's just what she did.

At the same time, Janette was having problems of her own. She loved being at the college at first and had chummed up with her room-mate called Rosie. Rosie was also a thalido-mide with much the same disabilities as Janette, except that she had little arms. Janette told me they took one look at each other and thought, "My God, what good are we going to be to each other!" But in fact they helped each other a lot. Rosie could do Janette's make-up with her hands and Janette could hold things for Rosie in her teeth. In the first few months Janette was full of the social events they'd been to, and their jaunts to the local pub. But then I noticed she was phoning home at least twice a week instead of once a month and I could tell from the catch in her voice that things weren't going so well. When she came home for a weekend the truth spilled out. She'd suddenly become aware of her disadvan-tages. Seeing other girls holding hands with their boyfriends had made her realise the importance of what she was missing. It must seem crazy that it had taken her sixteen years to find out she was disabled, but that's the truth of it. We were sitting at the kitchen table when she poured out her heart to me. "It's odd, mum," she said, "but until now being 'thalidomide' has just meant getting what I want, but it's not like that at all, is it?"

That was one of the most painful moments of my life. In a way Janette had always protected me from feeling guilty about taking that bloody drug. I'd explained to her about thalidomide as soon as she was old enough to understand and never once had she blamed me, even though she had a right to. She'd never moaned about being in a wheelchair or envied her brothers and sister. Quite the reverse, in fact, always being cheerful and making the best of her life. I knew she wasn't blaming me now but I felt guilty all the same. For the first time in her life she was feeling sorry for herself and so was I.

That weekend Janette said she thought she'd like to leave Hereward College. Several of her friends were suicidal, she said, and it was a depressing place to be. But we talked it through and she agreed that if Rosie stayed on so would she. It was the right decision because she picked herself up after that and became her normally cheerful self again. She finished her community care course and got a distinction in an English oral exam, and by the end of her second year she'd got O level passes in English literature and language, history and human biology.

Chapter 11

SHE'S LEAVING HOME

We were all so proud of Janette, especially her grandad. On her eighteenth birthday, on 24th April 1980, we announced her coming of age in the *Manchester Evening News* and held a huge party in her favourite nightclub. By this time, George and I had not so much broken up as come apart, but we were still mates and so he came along with his mum. Dad was there as well as Janette's friends from the Lancastrian and some from even further back. I'd spent weeks arranging it, going over the details in my mind, and I think for Janette it was the time of her life.

For me, though, it was a horrible experience. Dad was now ill with cancer and had grown very frail but he was determined to be at the party to watch his favourite granddaughter open her presents and be toasted in champagne. Unfortunately, Janette had no time for a sick old man when there were so many people of her own age around, and she didn't speak to him all evening. I could see how hurt he was and I spent most of the evening trying to explain that she was only eighteen, over-excited and thoughtless and that naturally she'd be concentrating on the friends of her own age. I think I finally persuaded him not to worry about it when I said that children were always taking their parents and relations for granted, just as I had with him and mum. But it was hard to sound convincing when inside I was seething with anger at the hurt being done to dad.

Once again in my life I felt split in two directions. I desperately wanted to have dad at home with me so that I could look after him properly but I knew this got on Janette's nerves. After the birthday party she came back home to Wordsworth Road, watching a lot of TV during the day and clubbing it in the evenings. There was always one of her mates who'd bring her home and stay overnight. The house was becoming more and more like Manchester Piccadilly station with teenagers of all sorts and sizes coming and going. I quite enjoyed the bustle of it, and it was great for Janette, but it was exhausting. I used to go round counting heads in the morning to find out how many breakfasts I had to cook. The generally good-natured commotion made me think how nice family life was, but it wasn't the family it should have been. Hayley was still away in what they call "a community home with education" and Karl was always buzzing off to play cricket or kick a ball around somewhere. As far as he was concerned I was just the launderette lady.

I'd missed out on so much of my kids' lives when they were small, and now just when there were things I wanted to do with them, and the time to do it, they were big enough to start leaving the nest. Neil had been the first one to fly off on his own. When he started misbehaving I told him to live by my rules or get out, and he got out. On the night before he was due to leave home to join the army he begged me to come and see him off the next day. How stupid can parents be? Sheer bloody-minded stubbornness wouldn't even let me say goodbye to him, let alone go and see him off. I couldn't altogether blame him for his feelings and behaviour towards me and I should have been big enough to cope with his anger, but I was too drained to handle anything well at the time – to my lasting regret. Fortunately, Neil turned out to be bigger than me. I tried not to make the same mistake with the others. There wasn't much I could do about Hayley, but I clung on to Janette and Karl by giving them as much freedom as they wanted.

Janette decided to do more studying and this time she went to South Trafford college nearer home. She needed someone to be there all day and help with the everyday things, like going to the toilet or getting her wheelchair up and down steps, which are part of the daily struggle for disabled people. I'd got my own job, on a night-shift in a hospital, and my own identity, which I didn't want to give up and so we persuaded a friend to become Janette's carer. Jane was a friend of Janette's and the college agreed to let her have a place. The only problem was that this girl was totally neurotic. If ever there was a problem she wouldn't come calmly and ask me to sort it out. She'd throw a complete wobbler. She'd stamp and screech. If it happened at home I'd say, "For God's sake sit down, stop bawling and tell me what it's all about!" We'd usually manage to work things out, but it was always such a waste of everyone's time. She'd be worried that the college work was too hard for her, or that people were laughing at her, or Janette was being too demanding. I'd reassure her and off she'd go quite happy again. But one day I got a phone call from college saying that Jane had thrown a terrible tantrum during a legal studies seminar, and walked out leaving Janette sitting there with no-one to help her and no-one to bring her home.

I was furious because I saw my independence in danger. Luckily the girls in Janette's group rallied round and told her she wasn't to worry because they'd take turns at looking after her, but this still left me with a problem at night when I was out at work. I was starting to panic until I remembered Sandra, who was willing to help out. She cost me five pounds a night, six cans of Carlsberg, her supper and a taxi home in the morning, but it was worth it to keep on with my own life.

For a while things truckled along merrily enough, with Janette getting on well at college, Karl handing me amazing amounts of dirty sports gear and dad squaring up to his illness. He had been at Christie's Cancer Hospital but the chemotherapy was taking too much out of him and eventually we agreed that he'd be better off without it, so he came home to Wordsworth Road. Then one afternoon Neil was standing on the doorstep asking if he could spend his Christmas leave with us. He said he would have rung first but he was afraid that would have given me a chance to reject him – again. It was so good to see him standing there, looking gorgeous in his uniform and with a kitbag full of presents, that I could only stand and stare at him with tears of delight rolling down my face. We hadn't spoken for several months and we were still stiff with each other but at least I hadn't forgotten how to hug and squeeze him. All the bad times when he'd been insolent or come home drunk or treated me like a doormat, they all evaporated and I felt nothing but pride. "Who is it?" shouted dad. "It's your grandson!" I called out to him. Dad's face, pitifully thin by this time, lit up with happiness when Neil walked into the lounge. I think by now he'd transferred the affection he'd once felt for Janette onto Neil and he was always boasting about his soldier grandson. Janette, on the other hand, didn't even say hello to her brother. "So, the prodigal son's returned!" was her only remark. In spite of that, it was a great Christmas.

The doctors had given dad less than a year to live. He was in constant pain and spent long periods in bed. To Janette he was an intrusion. Whenever he wanted something done for him, she'd call out for something else. If I went to him first because his need was greater, she'd get mad. I remember standing in the corridor one evening between their two rooms, having to shout out "Dear God! I know you've got no arms, Janette, but I've only got one bleeding pair. I can't see to you both at once and at the moment he gets priority here." Then I went into dad's room and his face was turned to the wall. "What is it you want, chuck?" I asked. The tears were rolling down his face and, God help me, I could have cracked Janette. There were so many times in those last weeks of my dad's life that I just wanted to give her one almighty whack across the face. She behaved as if her grandad was being ill on purpose to stop her having the things she wanted. She started turning on me, saying "This is my house, you know!" and it made me think of dad's warning when we first thought of moving to Wordsworth Road. "You may be living in a council house, now," he'd said, "but at least it's your name on the rent-book."

With Sandra virtually living with us half the time, spending the nights closeted in Janette's room drinking and gossiping, I used to hope that she might contribute something to family life. Some hope. She never once asked dad, for instance, if she could do anything for him. I used to go off to work leaving him with a flask of brandy and the district nurse would pop round and see him. But I'd always drive up to the house in the morning with a sense of dread. I was terrified that something had happened to him in the night when I wasn't there. The strain was tremendous so I asked for some time off work. I told Sandra I'd be home so she needn't worry about Janette for a while but she said she'd like to carry on all the same. I was a bit taken aback because she wasn't exactly creamy with the milk of human kindness. I suppose I was also disappointed because I was becoming worried about the influence she seemed to be having on Janette. Perhaps it was part of growing up but I noticed that Janette's language was becoming vile. One morning after I had got in from the hospital she told me to fuck off. "Since when have you been using language like that!" I demanded, but she just repeated it.

Shaking, I made my way downstairs and looked in on dad. He was in the room which had Janette's lift in it. It was boxed off in one corner but sounds tended to travel down from Janette's room. "Is she having a go at you again?" he said, but I just shrugged. "Well, I don't know what goes on up there when you're out at nights," dad went on, "but there's a lot of snickering and whispering and they're always on the phone. There's something not very nice about the pair of them though I can't put my finger on it. All I know is that Janette's changed, and I don't like who she is any more."

My old friend Anne, from the Calie days, was a regular visitor during dad's illness and she used to say the same thing. Janette had never much liked Anne because she was always one for plain-speaking. Once when Janette was in a mood and announcing that she wanted this and she wanted that, Anne had looked at her and said, "You know your trouble, young lady? You're frustrated, that's what you are!" Janette had never forgiven her, though if that was the worst that was ever said to her she should consider herself very fortunate. But like it or not, Janette had to put up with Anne's company for a few weeks while she scrambled round helping me look after dad and keep myself from falling apart with grief and anxiety. There was no love lost between Anne and Sandra, either. I'd told Anne that, although it must sound as if I was paranoiac, I couldn't help feeling there was some sort of conspiracy going on in Janette's room. "I go in and they shut up. It's as if they're plotting something." Anne said I should tell Sandra to get lost, but I explained that, as Janette never tired of saying, it wasn't my house and I had no right to choose her friends.

To ease the strain for a while, and give dad better nursing care, we booked him into a convalescent home in Blackburn for a few weeks. Then I got a phone call saying that he had fallen and broken his femur and was being taken into Blackburn General. I was chatting to him after the operation he'd had to insert a pin in the bone, when he said that, for my sake, he wanted to become a Catholic. I was surprised but glad and I went to see my parish priest that afternoon.

For days on end dad had been reminding me that it was Neil's passing-out parade soon and that I must make sure everyone got to it. He obviously wasn't able to make it to the ceremony in Northampton himself but the rest of us all planned to go, even Hayley who was about to be allowed out of her community home. Then Janette announced that she was going to stay with Sandra instead. I didn't have the energy to argue with her. "All right," I said, "if that's what you want, you go to Sandra's," and I didn't mention the matter again.

I'd promised to bring dad lots of photographs of Neil but I managed to do one better than that because Neil came back from the parade with us and the first thing we did was go and see dad, who was now in a nursing home in Gorton. Neil showed dad an award he'd won. He'd ruptured himself during training but had carried on regardless. I don't think dad could have been more pleased if Neil had been made a general, which was probably what the other patients thought had happened after hearing him crow so loudly. He was simply bursting with pride over his grandson. I think it must have made up for some of the disappointment I had caused him when I was younger, as if I couldn't be all bad by giving him someone like Neil. I felt pretty proud of him myself.

Five days later, I spent the morning with dad in Manchester Royal Infirmary, because the pin in his leg had worked itself out. After that I went home to have a bath and wash my hair. I'd just poured myself a drink and sat down when something told me to go back to the hospital. I rang the ward and asked the sister how he was. "Are you sure he's not got any worse?" I said, but she assured me he was about the same. I still had a weird feeling and so I phoned Anne who said she'd get over to the MRI, and I took a taxi there. I couldn't wait for the lift so I puffed up the stairs to the ward and found dad fighting for breath. He seemed in incredible pain. He'd been on quite high doses of pethidine but appeared not to have received any for some time. But although the staff could ease his agony, it was clear his time had come. I had my arms round him and he told me how much he loved me but that he had to leave me now. I had been there with him for twenty minutes before he died.

I don't know how long I stayed there holding him but two nurses came and led me away. I started screaming for someone to fetch a priest, and eventually dad was given the last rites. Anne arrived to fetch me home and we called George who'd been up to see dad the night before. Dad had given him his watch. When we got home I gave the children the news at once. They were eating some sandwiches in front of the television and when they heard they simply collapsed in tears, except Janette, who carried on watching the TV cartoons.

Dad's funeral was a few days later and thanks to Anne it was a good send-off. Neil wore his uniform and carried the coffin with George and two other friends. I was too upset to know much about what was going on. When we got back to the house I wanted everyone to go away so that I could cry my heart out without attracting sympathy and words of consolation. I was also hiding from something else. Janette had arranged to leave home on the day of the funeral. She had her cases packed before we drove to the cemetery and had arranged for a car to come along afterwards and take her and her luggage to Sandra's maisonette in Hulme. It was four years before I saw her again. I don't think we even said goodbye.

Janette waited until I was out of the house before coming back for the rest of her stuff. I tried phoning her but she wouldn't speak to me. I wrote her letters and sent her cards on her birthday and at Christmas, but never had a word in reply. Soon after she'd moved out, I had a letter from the trust telling me that in the circumstances I could either rent the house in Wordsworth Road or move out. I had no right to live there now that Janette was gone. I couldn't possibly afford the rent so it looked as if Karl and I would be made homeless. By this time Hayley had buzzed off again and was living in various squats around Manchester.

The other kids were outraged by Janette's behaviour. Neil and Karl each went to see Janette at Sandra's to plead with her not to have me turned out, but there was no changing her mind. I was desperately hurt and unhappy but I can't say I blamed her for what she did. It was yet another bid for independence. As she saw it, Neil had left home at sixteen without anyone making a fuss and here was she, at eighteen years of age, doing exactly the same. Why should she feel guilty about fleeing the nest like every other grown-up child? The fact that it meant her mother and youngest brother were tipped out of the tree as well was just coincidental bad luck and nothing to do with her.

I discovered later another reason for Janette leaving. During one of the whispering evenings in her bedroom, Sandra had given her the piece of information I'd left out when I told her and Neil about my time in Holloway. She told her that I'd had a choice and could have avoided prison by shopping Calie as my pimp. That had condemned me once and for all in Janette's eyes. I hadn't gone to prison and left her in Alder Hey because I was stupid or unlucky enough to get caught, I'd gone because I'd put my feelings for Calie before my feelings for her. Knowing this, she lost the little respect she had left for me.

I had little enough respect for myself by now. With both my dad and Janette gone I'd lost the two people who needed me most. As long as I could care for them, even if it meant running from one room to another fetching and carrying, I had some worth. Now I looked round and there was nothing about my life that had any value. The man I really loved had deserted me, I'd pushed out George, Neil had left home as soon as he could, and Hayley was a complete basket-case. Even my nursing seemed to have little value at the moment. Karl and I were still close but I wasn't sure how long it would be before he went the same way as the others. Once again I reached for the bottle. If I had been floating on booze before George had dried me out, now I was drowning in it. I'd guiltily sneak a drink as soon as I woke up in the morning. About a week after getting the letter from the trust, I sat down in the lounge one evening with a bottle of whisky and a load of tablets and downed the lot. I'd have snuffed it if a friend hadn't called round unexpectedly and found me sprawled on the settee. I was rushed into hospital where they pumped out my stomach and called for Neil, who was given compassionate leave from his regiment. Then, because I refused to say that I wouldn't try to kill myself again, they transferred me to a psychiatric hospital. That was truly terrible. It brought back horrific memories of my mother surrounded by potty old women and I was frightened that I'd never get out. I started crying as soon as I arrived and I don't think I stopped till I left six days later. I was rescued, yet again, by Anne who was willing to take me home with her and make sure I didn't do anything daft. Anne is the kindest woman I've ever met. She gave a home to me and Karl for a while and then took me along to the council housing department. They agreed to rehouse me in Sale, on the road out to Manchester Airport.

Little did I know it but at about the same time Janette's physical and mental health was also going downhill. She'd started by having a smashing time with Sandra, drinking and going out to clubs and bars without having to account to anyone for where she'd been. Sandra was a bit younger than me and very slim and fashion conscious. "Groovy" is how Janette once described her. Soon after Janette moved in, Sandra told her she was too fat and started her on a diet. She had a ten-year-old boy called Craig and he and Janette got on well enough, but then Sandra became pregnant again and Janette found herself doing more and more babysitting and less clubbing around town. Gradually it became a chore for Sandra to take her out. It even became a chore for Sandra to help her dress nicely or get in and out of the shower. She didn't get much to eat either and went down from ten stone to six – not that that was any bad thing.

As well as being kept a virtual prisoner, Janette was being ripped off financially. She gave Sandra seventy pounds a week for shopping, and often she'd let her draw money from her bank account, but I can't believe she cost Sandra that much in housekeeping. The trouble was that Janette was a sitting target. Hayley visited her sometimes and after one of these visits Janette found that her cheque book was missing. She called the police and Hayley was arrested. I suppose it wasn't surprising, given Hayley's track record, but the evidence was circumstantial. Neil and Karl couldn't believe that Janette would put her own sister in jail and begged her not to give evidence. Once again their pleas fell on deaf ears and Hayley was sent to Risley for nine months.

The two boys came back and told me what was going on. They were too angry with Janette to realise what a state she was in but I guessed something was up from their descriptions of her appearance and the slovenly condition of the house. By this time she'd been there for almost two years and she'd made no attempt to get in touch with me so I wasn't sure what I could do to help. Then I had an idea. I rang the social services and told them my daughter was being neglected. I asked all my friends at work to do the same and we hassled them with regular calls.

When Janette was younger she had been a devout Catholic and the priest would come to our house on Sundays to give her mass. Now she started going to the Mormon Church when she could persuade Sandra to get her up and ready in time. She chummed up with a woman called Maureen who suspected that Janette was being ill-treated and made her own call to social services. Meanwhile, I'd threatened to go to the Press with the story and all in all we managed to get some action. It was just as well, because by this time Janette was hardly going out of the house. In fact she'd vegetated completely. On some days she didn't get out of bed and she didn't wash. She just lay there watching videos. Now, though, a social worker visited Janette and persuaded her to attend the Frank Taylor day centre for the disabled. A car was sent for her each morning and she spent the day in company, had a good midday meal and began to perk up.

The social worker also introduced her to Oakwood Lodge, a residential unit for adults where you could have your own room and there were carers on duty twenty-four hours a day. She went to stay there under the pretence of giving Sandra a short break, then when Sandra came to collect her she refused to leave. She said she'd pay Sandra the usual shopping money for the next four weeks but that was it. Sandra was absolutely livid. It was coming up to Janette's twenty-second birthday and she threatened to come over with a birthday cake and shove it down her throat till she choked but there was no way she could persuade Janette to come back.

Of course I didn't know any of these details at the time. For four years I kept on ringing Sandra's number and praying that Janette would answer. I might have been a beggar asking for charity the way Sandra dismissed me, telling me that my daughter didn't want to have anything more to do with me. Whenever any of the kids had seen Janette I'd wring every little detail of the visit out of them afterwards. I wanted to know how she looked, what she was eating, wearing, what she was doing and who she was in touch with. But they stopped going after the business with Hayley and the cheque book so then my sources of information dried up completely.

I'd reached rock-bottom with that suicide attempt and from then on the only way out was upwards. It was work that helped me pull through. I had got a job in a centre for drug addicts and was able to put all my worst experiences to good use. I was quite good at drawing people out, getting them to talk about their experiences, and some of the kids at the unit had some terrible tales to tell. It made me realise my life wasn't so bad after all. To help them overcome their addiction I had to show that I could overcome my own and there was no way I could go back to drinking a bottle of gin or vodka a day. Anne helped again by pointing out that most of the booze I was drinking was made by Distillers!

I'd made some good friends at work and was back in control of my life. Me and Karl were very companionable although he was beginning to hang round with the wrong crowd in Manchester and I suspected he was smoking cannabis. On the whole, though, life was on an even keel. Then one morning, out of the blue, the phone rang and there was Janette on the other end. You could have knocked me over with a champagne cork. "I've run away," she said without another word of explanation. "What do you mean, run away?" I gasped. "How the heck can you run away without any frigging legs?" She just said that she'd left Sandra and was living in a fantastic place called Oakwood Lodge. She had her own room with a colour television and her own quilt and pictures and she was free. She didn't even have to pay anyone. It wasn't the time to ask her why she hadn't responded to any of the presents or cards I'd sent over the last four years. I knew that if I wanted to mend our relationship I'd have to swallow a lot of things that I'd like to say to Janette. When Janette asked if she could come round and see me, I said I'd ask the other kids and think about it. Karl said I should go ahead and see her but the others told me I shouldn't have anything more to do with her. I thought I was being democratic about it, but finally I thought stuff all that nonsense – she's my child and I'm desperate to see her!

Karl didn't want to be there when Janette came round for a meal at Sale. He thought the least she should do was apologise for what she'd done, but I tried to explain the situation from Janette's point of view and he agreed to stay in. It turned out to be a very strained meeting and I made a complete mess of the cooking. None of us knew quite what to say to each other, so we kept to small-talk, but it felt good to have her with us again. She had put on some of the weight she'd lost at Sandra's but she still looked thin to me and I could tell from her face that she'd packed in quite a lot of growing up in the four years since leaving Wordsworth Road. When she was about to go I arranged to visit her at Oakwood Lodge a few days later. I think the care assistants were surprised to see that she had a mother who was nothing like Sandra but was actually pleasant and cheerful. We were both much more relaxed this time and we managed to make a start on repairing the damage. All this time I was waiting to go into hospital for an operation on my bowel. It was a pretty serious operation and I stayed in for several weeks. What amazed and thrilled me was that Janette came to visit me every day and this finally undid all the harm which had been done to us by Sandra.

Chapter 12

SECOND TIME AROUND

In this life you win one and you lose one. I had Janette back now but I seemed to be losing Neil again. He had married Christine, a nice girl from Newark near Nottingham. Her family wanted all of us to come to the wedding but in the end only I went to stand by Neil. Christine's family had booked me and Karl into a hotel, but the little stinker had decided at the last minute that he didn't want to go to some fancy wedding. I'd have enjoyed it a bit more if I'd had him there for support. When I got back home to Sale, feeling pretty limp and wondering how I was going to keep my end up with Neil's in-laws, Karl popped into the kitchen and said, "Hi mum. How did the wedding go?" In a flash of anger I was anything but limp as I socked him so hard across his smirking face that he crashed to the floor. After Neil's marriage, we saw less and less of him. As for Hayley, she came and went but I dreaded her comings more than her goings. She'd turned into a real junkie and had contracted Hepatitis B. When my colleagues at work heard about this they asked me to bring in my own cup and my own knife and fork in case I was contagious.

Janette was still living at Oakwood Lodge and going to the Frank Taylor day centre. For a break from the day centre, though, she used to go to Withington's Young Disabled Unit and it was here that she met Bob. He was quite a bit older than she was and he was there because his wife Bridget had chucked him out after it was discovered that he had multiple sclerosis. When he wasn't welding things together, Bob could usually be found forming bonding relationships with pubs! Multiple sclerosis gave him periods of normality when he was perfectly fit and able to walk around and drive a car, and others when he could hardly move and had to stay in hospital.

Janette took an immediate shine to him and I think it was her who made the suggestion outright that they should go to bed together. It was odd that she should light on another victim. Sickness is a great leveller but Janette always preferred able-bodied types. Anyway, Bob was able enough because he used to stay overnight with Janette at Oakwood Lodge, adding "Man At Work" to the Do-not-Disturb sign on Janette's bedroom door.

For Christmas 1985 I flew to Belfast because I was keen to see Neil and Christine again, and they were stationed there with his regiment. Two days before I was due to arrive, Christine had dashed back home to see her mum, who had just been diagnosed as having leukemia and who died before Christmas was over. On New Year's Eve I phoned Janette for a Christmassy sort of chat but she wasn't saying much. I babbled on and then she interrupted me. "Mum, I'm not sure if you want to know this, but I think I'm pregnant."

It's difficult to describe how I felt about it. For a start, I'm not sure I believed her, especially as she was only a fortnight late with her period. (Bob didn't believe her either. It took a proper pregnancy test to convince him.) But there was more to it than that. When she had been operated on as a child, to remove her appendix, they'd told me she had everything there in the right places so I should have known it was possible. But this was the child they'd said would never live, never grow up to be a woman. Now here she was on New Year's Eve telling me she was expecting a baby of her own.

For me it was a new beginning. I felt wild with happiness and Neil had to hold me back from buzzing off to the nearest Mothercare store. Married life was obviously doing Neil good because even he was prepared to admit that it was exciting news. I'd been ringing home for a few days, trying to talk to Karl, but without any luck. I called a neighbour on the off-chance and she said that she was sorry to have to be the one to mention it but that we had been burgled. Neil managed to get me on a flight back to Manchester the next day. There was no sign of Karl but the place looked as though Hurricane Hayley had hit it. I checked the drawer in my bedroom where I kept a few good bits of jewellery and cash for emergencies. Everything of any value had gone and I immediately thought of Hayley, who'd been allowed out of jail, and had obviously come round looking for money to beg or steal. I was about to phone the police and let them know I was there when Karl turned up. He was a pathetic sight, thin and ill-looking. I could tell from his eyes that he'd been taking more than cannabis and I sat him down and forced the truth out of him. Hayley had indeed come out of prison but she hadn't stolen from me – not money, anyway. She'd done far worse than that by introducing her baby brother to heroin. Karl had taken the money for supplies. I could have slashed my wrists then and there, and perhaps I would have done if it hadn't been for Janette's news and the fact that she probably needed me now more than ever.

Karl stayed at home though he'd disappear for days on end. Sometimes the police came looking for him and one day he woke up to find a gun pointing in his face. It was the serious crime squad, who'd been led up the garden path by a tip-off from Hayley. He was also suspected of drug dealing and arrested but the drug squad didn't find enough evidence to bring a charge. I'd done enough grieving for Hayley and I tried to harden my heart to what was happening to Karl. But he was a grand lad, kind and considerate, and we'd been very close over the last few years. It was impossible not to live in fear that he'd be sent to prison or found dead in some toilet from an overdose.

More and more I tried to turn my attention to Janette and Bob. By now Bob's parents had been told about the pregnancy and I'm sorry to say they didn't share my delight. Still, that wasn't surprising. Not only had their son got multiple sclerosis and his large family had broken up but he'd taken up with a younger woman with no arms or legs and then got her pregnant. It had all come out when Bob's father went to visit him in hospital during one of his bad spells. Janette was determined that Bob's dad should know, but Bob was too much of a coward and disappeared to the day room. Janette then told her future father-in-law about her and Bob in her characteristically forthright fashion. He listened in silence and then said, "I didn't hear that and I'm certainly not telling the wife." But his wife Maisie found out soon afterwards because she saw Janette throwing up one morning and her first thought was "What'll Bob's wife and his kids think?" She was naturally enough more concerned about Bob's first family, his wife Bridget and her four grandchildren, than about Janette and the baby on its way.

Of course I had to meet the parents. They lived in a very respectable suburb in a house with smart furniture that looked as if it was polished every day and dust-free china ornaments, all neatly arranged. As soon as Maisie got me alone in the kitchen she asked me what I thought about Janette being pregnant. I told her I could understand if she had reservations but I was absolutely delighted. "Well," she huffed, "I think it's disgusting!" and she looked as if she was about to be sick all over the gleaming vinyl floor. She made it quite clear that this baby, if baby it turned out to be and not some monster, was nothing to do with her side of the family. In a flash I saw myself back in Mrs Henry's front room, cradling Janette in my arms. This was another grandchild who was going to be disowned, but not by me.

The first antenatal appointment was like a family day out. Normally it's just the expectant mum who goes along, but on this occasion Janette went, Bob went and I went too. Even though the pregnancy had been confirmed by her GP, the hospital doctors said the only way they could be certain was to give her a scan, which they did. There we were afterwards with official confirmation – the same slip of paper everyone else has, and we were off. As we left the hospital we turned to each other and simultaneously yelled out "We're having a baby!" Passers-by must have thought we were completely cracked. But in the months that followed anyone would have thought it was me having the baby. I think I went through every ache, pain and sickness with Janette. In fact I think I suffered more discomfort than she did and I certainly complained more on her behalf. She didn't moan once, even though the extra weight was extremely difficult to bear for someone as large as Janette and unable to move around on her own two feet.

After the initial excitement we came down to earth and

discussed the possibility of anything being wrong with the baby. The hospital had said they wouldn't know for certain about this for another couple of months. We discussed the horrible word "termination" and Bob and Janette were sure they couldn't handle a handicapped child, in which case there would have to be an abortion. If the baby was born mentally handicapped they agreed they'd have to leave it in hospital and put it up for adoption, though I'd have been in a real fix because I don't think I could have abandoned my grandchild. These were hard decisions to make, but there were too many factors already against them as new parents and it was no good burying our heads in the sand.

In April Janette went off for another scan and she was told that though the baby was small it appeared healthy in all other respects and so our days of anticipating the worst were over. Janette was making medical history, and the hospital staff were being particularly helpful in keeping us in the picture. The first thing we did was go off on a mammoth spending spree. We had a big estate car, plus a roof-rack, but even so I don't know how we managed to bring all the stuff home. We bought a pram, a high-chair, feeding equipment, teddy bears, disposable nappies, bedding for the cot. There was hardly room for Bob at the steering wheel let alone Janette and me when we took it all home. Janette couldn't keep it all at Oakwood Lodge so we had to store it at my place and I spent the next six months stumbling past piles of baby equipment.

No-one at Oakwood Lodge had ever got pregnant before and the management team didn't think they could handle the situation satisfactorily, excellent though they were, so Bob and Janette had to start searching for a home. The council offered them a house in Wythenshawe but it was mouldy with damp and not fit for a family of ducks to live in. There were diddicoys on one side and an empty house on the other so we told them what they could do with that. She could have bought another house but after the trouble at Wordsworth Road she'd sworn never to do that again. She didn't want Bob turned out on the streets if anything happened to her.

She and Bob were discussing the situation in the pub one lunchtime when a reporter from the *Manchester Evening News* overheard them. From that moment on Janette's pregnancy became the talk of the town. Suddenly it wasn't just her baby any more, and it wasn't just my grandchild, it belonged to the whole of Manchester. Everywhere we went, people were congratulating her and wishing her good luck. This was very cheering, and a great surprise to Bob, who had no experience of being in the public eye, but most usefully I think that the media attention helped them find a decent house in a good area. We'd been hammering away at the housing department for all we were worth and now all of a sudden they came up with the perfect house. Her rehabilitation officer took her to see a three-bedroomed house in Barcicroft Road in Burnage, which she fell in love with right away.

It needed a lot of work doing on it and Bob and I set to cleaning it up and redecorating. Bob had got his divorce in May, on the same day that Prince Andrew and Fergie got married, but we had to wait before it was made absolute. Of course we were anxious that the baby should be born in wedlock but it was touch and go till the end. We'd already had one go at arranging the wedding. A hall had been booked for 21st June and I'd ordered the cake but Bob's ex-wife Bridget seemed to be holding things up. "That bitch of a wife!" Janette complained to me one day. "She won't go to court so my bleeding wedding's down the drain!"

Poor Janette. It was summer and she was the size of a doubledecker bus. If ever we went shopping now, we had to be careful not to buy too much because with her in the car there wasn't room for more than a few parcels. She was also getting impossibly heavy to manoeuvre in and out of doorways, and even the ramps which were appearing in more and more places seemed to become steeper every week. I always went with her to the antenatal clinic and the doctors said everything was progressing normally but I was getting angry with them. (I wasn't just picking on the doctors – although I was very happy I was also so tense with nervous excitement that I was getting angry with everyone!) On one visit the nurses couldn't get Janette onto the examination table. The more they tried the more flustered they all became and it turned into a real farce. There was a period when she never seemed to see the same doctor twice. One after another disappeared leaving a new one who'd have to poke and prod Janette all over again, asking the same questions and making the same jokes. I felt as though she was being treated like a strange medical exhibit, a source of exotic fascination to the experts and it reminded me of my own painful dealings with gynaecologists and obstetricians.

To help make up for the delayed wedding, Bob and I decided to take Janette to Butlins in Minehead for a week. There was a sing-song in the theatre one evening and Bob put Janette's name down for a solo. When she learnt what Bob had done I thought she was going to boff him, but she pulled herself together and went out to show him what she could do. She sat on the platform in her wheelchair and the compère told the audience that she was pregnant, as if they couldn't see it for themselves, and how marvellous it was, and how plucky she was, and so on. By this time I was ready to thump Bob myself for the embarrassment he was putting us through but then Janette launched into her distinctive rendering of the Everly Brothers' song "All I Have to do is Dream". Janette is unlikely to win the Eurovision Song Contest but she hasn't got a bad voice, and I felt very proud of her, up on stage and pouring out the song, and couldn't help shedding a few tears.

Bob's divorce finally came through in July, when Janette was seven months pregnant. The moment we got the news we headed for the register office in Jackson's Row. Then we realised we'd never get Janette up the steps so Bob and I went inside leaving her in the car. Bob was showing the registrar his divorce papers and we were discussing possible dates for the wedding when it suddenly clicked that the man thought it was me and Bob who were getting married. After all, he's only a few years younger than me. We straightened that one out and Bob explained that his real wife-to-be was disabled and waiting for us in the car. The registrar, looking a bit flushed by this time, came outside with papers for Janette to sign. He looked at the size of her and said, "How about three weeks from today?"

Now the panic really set in. I chased around Manchester

organising the invitations, ordering flowers, arranging the catering. Bob and I spent every available moment working on the house. And, of course, there was Janette's wedding dress to buy. We set off for central Manchester determined to find something as pretty as we could for a bride who was by now eight months pregnant. Just as we were getting out of the car, Janette let out an almighty scream and we thought that was it, she was in labour. How we got her from there to Withington Hospital I'll never know. Bob drove the car very slowly and I held on to Janette, who was half on, half off the seat, immobile with pain and furious about not getting her wedding dress. I'd managed to phone the hospital to warn them and a doctor and two nurses were waiting at the steps to the maternity department.

She wasn't in labour after all but the baby was lying on the sciatic nerve and the hospital decided to keep her in. We were hoping and praying they'd allow her out for the wedding, which was arranged for 13th August. With one week to go the hospital said that she could have the day out as long as she was back by ten the next morning. It was like being married under a curfew. We held the hen night in the maternity ward and Janette's bed was surrounded by female friends and relations. Goodness knows what the other patients thought was going on because we must have made a terrible racket, especially when the stripogram arrived dressed like a vicar. He was really gross, with breath that sent you reeling, but somehow that only made it funnier when he tried to lunge at Janette. Eventually the nurses had to turn us all out and Janette was mad at being deprived of a real party. She'd told Bob that if she couldn't go out on her hen night, he wasn't to go out on a stag night either, and before I left the hospital she made me promise to present him in good shape at the wedding the next day. That looked as if it might be a problem. Unknown to Janette, Bob had been spending the evening with some mates at a hotel in the city centre. He and his daughter Sarah were staying at my house in Sale, and I picked him up, pissed as a newt, on my way back. As soon as we got home the phone was ringing and it was Janette checking that he'd obeyed her instructions and spent a sober evening in front of the television. I kept her chatting while Sarah forced two cups of black coffee down her dad and we plonked him in an armchair and gave him the phone, glad that Janette couldn't see the human wreck at the other end.

Next day a friend from Oakwood Lodge took Janette from the hospital to Jackson's Road register office. As they drove up they saw Bob in the car ahead, just managing to make it to the wedding before his bride. There was a line of Press photographers waiting and the journalist from the *Daily Mirror* who'd bought Janette's story. Janette was wearing a black and white dress and I thought she looked lovely but she thought she looked hideous. She asked them not to print her picture in the papers but they went ahead all the same and I suppose it was news so you can't blame them. Bob and Janette were going to exchange rings, and Janette had hers on a chain round her neck. I remember wondering how she was going to take it in her mouth and say "With this ring I thee wed" at the same time, but she got round the problem somehow and emerged from the ceremony Mrs Janette Cooke. From the registry office we went to Oakwood Lodge where they'd organised a small party and then the main reception was at a restaurant nearby. Maisie had looked pretty sour throughout the wedding, but as we steadily filled her to the brim with booze she relaxed and got a bit merrier. She even managed a wave when Bob and Janette left for their wedding night in the Excelsior Hotel.

A wedding night when you're on the verge of giving birth and your new husband's having one of his bad turns with MS isn't much fun. Afterwards they managed to joke about it, which I thought was quite an encouraging start to their married life. I think they managed a few hours sleep but that was all. In the morning Bob drove Janette back to the maternity ward.

She was in hospital seven weeks altogether before the birth, becoming more and more nervous. They'd told her the baby would be small, which would make things easier. But because she was Rhesus-negative there was every chance she'd need a blood transfusion and there was a lot of discussion about the best way to put her on a drip. It was decided she'd have to have it in the side of her neck. Janette's always been terrified of needles and she immediately announced that she was having nothing done without her mum there.

I'd given up my job by this time, realising there was more than enough work to be done at home. And in any case, I had enough drug addiction in my own family to live with and resolve without taking on the community's cares as well. I was in and out of the hospital with shopping for Janette and so many extras for the baby that the staff nurse thought they'd need to build a new maternity wing just to store it. We'd bought everything we needed in the way of baby equipment but there were always luxuries to tempt me, like mobiles and booties and fluffy toys. Janette really needed cheering up by this time. She couldn't get out of bed, her hair was too long and I thought if she got any bigger she'd explode. I tried to keep her mind off the birth itself, but that was hard when it was the only thing I could think of day and night. When I wasn't in the hospital I was waiting for the phone to ring to tell me she was in labour, and I didn't dare leave my house for long in case it happened. The expected date of arrival was 29th August but it came and went and we were still hanging on.

At last, on 1st September, the phone call came. The maternity sister told me Janette's waters had broken and she'd squealed out "Fetch me mum!" I think what brought it on was that she'd been so fed up she'd tried getting in her wheelchair to leave the hospital. "Where've you bleedin' been?" she said when Bob and I dashed in. She was scared out of her wits. She was in labour and wired up to a monitor but at ten o'clock that night things just fizzled out and we were advised to go home and come back the following day. The doctors had a go at starting her off again at nine o'clock the next morning, which meant putting a drip in her neck. Again, it was her mum she wanted and I tried soothing her down while they put a needle in. There was a tiny bit of blood but Janette immediately thought they'd cut an artery or something. "Don't tell me if it's blood!" she moaned, feeling a trickle of wetness in her hair. "What is it?" she whimpered, and then the next moment, "For God's sake don't tell me what it is!"

Fourteen different doctors came to have a look at Janette while she was in labour. She was marvellous all the way through, and only let out a scream once at about seven o'clock that evening when she'd been in the labour ward for nine hours. She was determined to be awake to see her baby born but she was becoming exhausted. The doctor in charge was waiting for his professor to come back from London but at 9.15 p.m. the big chief rang to say he'd been delayed. They told him they couldn't leave Janette any longer because the baby was far down and pushing against her pelvic girdle, so he gave the go-ahead for a Caesarean section. By now Janette was beyond caring. When they'd given her the pre-med, she called for me and made me swear that I'd look after Bob if she and the baby died, and if the baby was all right, that I'd look after that as well.

I grabbed hold of an orderly who seemed to be scurrying around with the rest of them and begged her to keep us posted with what was going on, then Bob and I stationed ourselves near the theatre. The woman was true to her word. She kept coming in and out saying that the doctors were doing this and the doctors were doing that, so that when the nurse came out to tell us we had a baby girl in the family, we told her we already knew and she looked astonished. She said it would take a quarter of an hour to clean up the baby and bring her out to us, so Bob hurried off to telephone as many people as he could and I was left standing there with a ridiculously big grin all round my face.

Ten minutes later Bob was still not back and the doors of the operating theatre opened. The nurse came and put my granddaughter into my arms, wrapped tight in a blanket. She had chubby cheeks and fair hair and she looked the very image of her mother. Perhaps I should say that she looked the image of what I would have liked Janette to be. In my mind I was back twenty-four years before and I just sat cradling this baby with the tears pouring down my face. I cried then for the crying I didn't do all those years ago and they were tears of guilt and tears of happiness. The guilt was for the disappoint-ment I'd felt when Janette was born, and the fact that I hadn't wanted to see her or touch her. But now I knew that Janette would share the joy that any able-bodied mother could feel. It was as if God was giving us both a second chance. Nothing that happens to me, I thought, can ever overshadow this moment.

Janette hadn't trusted Bob to chose the right name, so she'd given him a shortlist of six names to pick from and he'd decided on Kelli-Anne. Kelli-Anne and I were alone together for more than ten minutes and during that time I made her a promise. "I'll always look after you, my darling," I said aloud. "As long as you need me, I'll always be there." When Bob came in I handed him his daughter but I was sure that, however delighted he was, he could never feel the same warm thrill that was glowing through my whole body.

The birth of my granddaughter couldn't have been more different from Janette's birth. There was no hiding this baby away from prying eyes. When the news got out, the whole of Manchester seemed to be celebrating. The Manchester newspapers and the local television news bulletins announced her birth: "The only child to be born to a woman with no arms and no legs." It was strange to have Janette described in that way, but it seems she'd made medical history.

The only people who weren't celebrating in those first few hours were Janette herself, and Maisie. Maisie sounded grudging and suspicious on the phone. "Is there anything wrong with it?" she wanted to know. I thought sadly that people's attitudes don't change as if by magic – they have to learn change. As for Janette, she was too ill to take much notice of her baby. The day after Kelli-Anne was born she was still in a great deal of pain. I was very worried about her because she looked so pale, as if all the life had drained out of her. I kept saying to the nurse, "Are you sure she's all right? She looks pretty ghastly to me!" but the staff didn't seem to know what to expect. It took three days for the doctors to realise that she was haemorrhaging, and she had to be given four pints of blood.

Once she regained her strength and vitality, the joy began to shine through. "This baby's mine," she said to me. "She's not even Bob's, she's mine. And she's achieved for me everything I haven't had for myself – my arms and legs!" It was maddening for her not to be able to do everything for Kelli-Anne herself. The Caesarean stitches were too painful to have the baby in a sling round her tummy, but she found a way of leaning her up between her flipper feet. Worst of all was the fact that she couldn't feed her at first and when the dummy fell out of Kelli-Anne's mouth she had to call me or a nurse to help put it back. She resented other people having to look after her baby, even Bob, although she never seemed to mind me doing things for her. She did have some moments of triumph, though. She had been upset because she was the only person who hadn't been able to buy something for Kelli-Anne. But one morning when the WRVS lady came round as usual with her trolley, Janette noticed she was selling a few soft toys as well as the magazines, soap and make-up and her eyes lit up when she saw a toy dog wearing dungarees. She bought it and asked for it to be put in the Perspex cot by Kelli-Anne's head. From that day on Kelli-Anne has never let that dog out of her sight. He's called Bimbo and he's the one toy she takes with her wherever she goes.

It was soon clear to me that although Bob was thrilled to be a father all over again, he wasn't over-anxious to be involved in every bottle-feed or nappy change. As this was his fifth baby it was understandable that the excitement had worn fairly thin. Still, it was my fifth baby too in a way, and it was a role Janette wanted me to have. Early on, she said, "Mum, you're going to have to be my arms and legs from now on." I think I'd prepared myself for this from that magnificent moment on New Year's Eve when she told me she was pregnant and I wouldn't have had it any other way. It really was my second chance.

Chapter 13

NANA

At about the same time that Kelli-Anne was being born, Hayley announced that she was going to have a baby as well. It would have been easy to think that there was a me-too element about it, except that Hayley couldn't even plan to make a cup of tea. Not only that, she was still filling herself with heroin and there was no question of coming off that in time to give her own baby much of a chance. The only time she attended an antenatal clinic was when I managed to catch her outside a pub one lunchtime and drag her off there. I had to pour her into the car, stoned out of her brains, and bundle her through the hospital doors. I'm not sure she even noticed her pregnancy but she had made me promise that I'd be with her when she went into labour. I agreed, of course, though more out of duty than love and it was just as well I was there. She was making one hell of a racket and I honestly think the staff would have thrown her out if I hadn't been able to calm her down a bit. As nothing had happened by midnight I popped home to put out Kelli-Anne's clothes for the morning, knowing that if I didn't there'd be total confusion when she woke up, with no-one knowing where to find things. It was the first night I'd been away from her and I realised how much we needed each other.

I'd only been back in the house about ten minutes when the phone rang. The sister from the labour ward was complaining that Hayley was demanding drugs and that some friends had appeared with a supply. I told her to hang on and I'd be right back, and by the time I arrived the baby had been born, a beautiful girl weighing five pounds. The midwife was expecting the baby, which Hayley named Regan, to have withdrawal symptoms. She was whisked into intensive care, but after seventy-two hours she was showing no signs, though she was pretty weak and had breathing problems.

The day after Regan was born, Karl was up before the judge on a burglary charge. He'd been on remand for six and a half months and now he was sentenced to nine months in prison, and sent to Strangeways. At least we were able to rally round him to some extent, because Bob and Janette came with me to give him what encouragement and support we could before he was sent down. I just thanked my lucky stars I had Janette and her family, and that Neil was happily settled. It stopped me from feeling a complete disaster as a mother, though only just.

Hayley took Regan back to the flat which she shared with Tony, the father, but soon afterwards she left him and got a place of her own. Then a friend of hers phoned me to say that she thought the baby was being neglected. Hayley was leaving her all day in her cot and slapping her when she cried, which of course was most of the time. I went over to see for myself and sure enough Regan was filthy, soaking wet, and wearing a nappy that she must have been in for days. I thought this was the sort of thing that people read about in their newspapers and here it was happening to my second granddaughter. I was relieved I'd managed to get there before social services. I called Janette and she said I should bring Regan home right away. I got hold of Tony and he agreed it was the best thing to do, so I asked the social services to put a place of safety order on the child until I could get the court to give me custody. Eventually Regan was made a ward of court and I was given care and control of her. Hayley was denied access to her, but Tony has always been very supportive and we arranged that he'd have her every other weekend.

As for Janette, after the birth of Kelli-Anne, she had stayed in hospital for three more weeks. That was a boring ordeal for her, but Bob and I needed every moment of it to finish getting the house in Barcicroft Road ready. I still don't know how we managed it in time, with all the coming and going to the Withington Hospital, our arms deep in disinfectant and polish and fuelled by lager and crisps. Finally we welcomed mother and daughter to a sparkling house, festooned with ribbons and a banner saying "Welcome Home Janette and Kelli-Anne".

Once they were both home and settled in, my life changed completely. Janette had proved she could be a mother by giving birth, and she was immensely proud of that. But now she had to face up to her limitations as a parent, and the painful fact that there were so many things she couldn't do for Kelli-Anne. Consequently I found myself with a new job. I became Janette's arms and legs in my new role as Kelli-Anne's Nana. It is the most satisfying and enjoyable job I've ever had, although for the first few months it was blooming hard work. She was a very unsettled baby. She never slept for long and she suffered from wind after every feed. It meant I was up and down all through the night seeing to her and because Janette couldn't bear to hear her cry I had to pick her up every few minutes during the day, which made her even more demanding. The funny thing was that I never ever got tired or lost my patience. Sometimes I forgot she wasn't my baby and Janette would have to tell me off. For Janette it was a very frustrating time.

The jobs that Janette could perform became all the more important. Once Kelli-Anne was on solids, Janette started to feed her and it was a painstaking process. It took about an hour for her to prepare the food in the kitchen. By gripping a long-handled spoon in her mouth, she'd manage to stir the milk and rice together in a dish. Then I'd sit on the sofa holding the baby as close as I could to Janette's wheelchair while she balanced the spoon in her mouth and held it to Kelli-Anne's lips. In an uncanny way Kelli-Anne seemed to sense her mother's difficulties. Janette would nurse her on her chest while I sat close by, and the little thing clung on, her tiny fingers clutching her mum's dress.

We got a lot of attention when we went out. People would come up and coo over Kelli-Anne and tell Janette how brave and splendid she was. There were only a few times when I wished they'd keep their remarks to themselves, like the time I overhead a couple of young mums: "It's disgusting that someone like that should even go to bed with a bloke, let alone have a baby!" As Kelli-Anne got older, Janette needed less help. The baby could sit in a high-chair to be fed, instead of in my arms, and as she got stronger she learned to climb onto Janette's chair and snuggle up close. In some ways I saw history repeating itself. She was as precocious a child as her mother had been. Instead of the gurgling noises other babies make, Kelli-Anne was virtually silent until she could form proper words and she learned to sit up and crawl much earlier than other children.

In April 1987, when Kelli-Anne was eight months old, we celebrated Janette's twenty-fifth birthday and the fact that she was now mistress of the small fortune that had been put in trust for her after the settlement with Distillers. It was an important occasion, and marked a growing maturity in Janette. From the time that she became directly responsible for her own money, she adopted a much more relaxed attitude towards it, which was very welcome after the stinginess of her teenage years. In fact she became very generous, though at the same time she was developing a shrewd business sense. One of the first things we all did after her birthday was to go on holiday to America. Janette had always wanted to go there and it was the first real break I'd had in years. We were both wide-eyed at all the new sights, all the things that before had only been a world of television and films. Bob loved it too, though he didn't fancy the American bars as much as the pubs of Manchester. What we enjoyed most was the warm friendliness of the Americans. They seemed so relaxed and unpretentious compared with people in England, who seem to be always showing off to each other. It was there that Kelli-Anne cut her first tooth and when I noticed it I called out the news to Bob and Janette who were walking a few yards ahead. Instantly a group of middle-aged Americans turned round and smiled in shared enjoyment. We made lots of friends in the States and they were all really interested in Janette and the story of thalidomide. All the Americans we met had the unusual, to us, gift of showing calm sympathy towards Janette's plight while responding to her as to any other human being.

It was after we got back that we had the sorry saga of Hayley and Regan on our hands, which was how I eventually came to have two babies to look after. I had their two cots beside my bed, with Kelli-Anne's bars down so that when she cried she could just crawl in with me. I'd wake up most mornings with her little blonde head peeping out of my duvet and her warm limbs curled up beside me. Regan was very easy and never woke, so in a way it was like having Janette and Neil all over again, the one demanding, the other placid.

When we first had Regan as a small baby, Janette found she was able to do things for her that she hadn't had the strength to do for Kelli-Anne. She could have Regan lying on a tray in front of her, ready to grab her with her teeth if she started to roll. She's given her niece a warm family home, taken on the financial responsibility and Regan thinks the world of her. Whenever the spotlight's on Kelli-Anne, for being the first baby born to a mother with no arms and legs, Janette makes sure that Regan gets a look in too. We so enjoyed our first American trip that we went again, taking both girls to see Disneyland. Since then we've also taken them to Tenerife and once I took them on my own for a holiday in Benidorm. That was a mistake. It seemed like a good idea at the time but I'd overlooked the fact that I wasn't quite as young as I felt and that there was a big difference between coping with a couple of toddlers in our own home and struggling with them single-handed in a foreign country. It left me with a hernia and I came home in agony!

Old or not, I'm the one who sees to most of the girls' everyday needs. I still put their clothes out in the morning, and get them their meals, and if they're sick it's me who mops up. Originally I planned to stay in Barcicroft Road until Kelli-Anne came off her night feeds. From the first moment she slept right through the night, I intended to go back to the flat of my own that Janette had bought me. But, because of Kelli-Anne's terrible sleeping patterns, that wonderful moment didn't come for two and a half years. By then of course I had Regan as well and our lives seemed tangled up so tightly they'd be difficult to untie. Years of taking them to playschool, dancing classes, skating, seeing to their birthday parties, wiping their tears, making them laugh, all adds up to a considerable relationship. Kelli-Anne and I have a very special bond and to Janette's credit she's never once shown any jealousy, even when Kelli-Anne learned to talk and started to call me mum. She soon learned who was really her mum but many times I forgot and Janette had to remind me I was Nana. I suppose even now I'm capable of behaving as if only I know what's best for Kelli-Anne.

As Kelli-Anne's got older she's obviously become more aware that her mummy isn't the same as her friends' mummies. At first she'd get a bit confused and hurt when Janette couldn't do simple things for her like tying her shoe-laces or doing up buttons, but now she understands and she's almost protective of her mum. When she meets someone new in the street she'll often pre-empt their surprise by declaring "My name's Kelli-Anne and my mum's got no arms or legs!" She's never been backwards coming forward, that little one. In fact she's got us all sorted out. If we're sitting round the table at teatime and Janette asks her to do something she doesn't want to do, she'll turn to me and say, "You're her mum, Nana, so you tell her I won't do it!" At first we thought this type of behaviour was hilarious but she's used it once too often. She's growing up to be quite a little manipu-lator and she's capable of playing the three adults off against each other. I have a great sense of responsibility for Regan because after all I've been put in the position of mother to her, and I can be strict if I have to, but with Kelli-Anne I'm as soft as butter. I find it hard to refuse her anything.

Janette now has a job on a hotel switchboard and she does shifts. When she's at home she has a carer who comes in and helps, but it's Bob who does all the fetching and carrying. He drives her to work and brings her back, and also goes into the hotel at least twice to take her to the toilet. Sometimes he'll drive Kelli-Anne and Regan to school and I'll pick them up. He must be one of the world's most patient men. Not many would put up with Janette's demands and my interference but he's the kind who'll do anything for anyone who needs him. I know I have been interfering at times because I can never keep my mouth shout if I think something's not right, but Bob and I keep and enjoy our friendship through thick and thin. His MS still takes him in and out of hospital but fortunately it's been in remission for the last four years.

In the last two or three years Janette's come more and more into her own as a mother. She spends hours reading to Kelli-Anne and helping her with jigsaws, and she's promised to get her a computer soon, which they'll both be able to use and play on. I used to think that I might be anxious about feeling eased out of the relationship as Kelli-Anne grew older and closer to Janette, but I'm glad to say that I don't. There was a moment when Kelli-Anne was about three and we were all out shopping in Stockport. We had one last toyshop to go to. It was a few blocks away and Bob and I decided to go in the car with Regan, but Janette said she preferred to make her own way there in the electric wheelchair. I was a bit worried when Kelli-Anne said she wanted to go with her mum because I wasn't sure she'd manage to walk that far and there were some busy roads to cross. But I was glad I'd managed to control myself and not say anything when I looked back and saw the expression of pride on Kelli-Anne's face. There she was, striding along beside her mum, with one hand on the arm of the chair. They got to a crossing and I watched the traffic-lights turn red and Janette hurry Kelli-Anne in front of her across the road. By the time we got to the shop they were already there, proud as Punch the pair of them. To be honest with myself, I have to say that I was rather dejected because I realised this was the first step towards my not being needed so much. But that feeling only lasted briefly and was far out-weighed by the pleasure of seeing mother and daughter basking in their sense of achievement.

I sometimes wonder now whether there'll come a time when I have to distance myself from the two of them but, with Bob's illness, I'm not sure this will be possible. I'd like to try spending more time at my flat in the centre of Manchester but I'm sure I'd miss them more than they'll miss me. I've centred my life around Janette and Kelli-Anne and as yet they show no sign of wanting it any other way. Janette's not really one to show her feelings, but of my four kids I know she's the only one who really understands me. To Hayley and Karl I'm the great provider, someone to come to when they're in trouble. Neil has made his own world, with the army and his own family, and I'm not really part it. I love being with him and his children, Dale and Janine, but his resentment of Janette and now also of Kelli-Anne is still a barrier between us. Janette and I don't have to talk to know what the other's thinking. We can be critical of each other without falling out. I can now think of Janette at any time and know that I've got rid of all my guilt at last.

Sometimes I wish I could cut and divide myself among all my children and grandchildren so that they could share me without being jealous of each other. I just want to make sure that with this new generation we can put things right. Before, when I was bringing up my own children, I felt as if I were riding a raft on the rapids and just couldn't get off. Now I'm trying to keep the raft slow and steady on the river so that, if things start going wrong, I can get us all off before we get hurt. I worry about Kelli-Anne becoming spoiled and Regan getting pushed out. I hear Kelli-Anne making demands and other people giving in to her, and I watch Regan misbehaving as a way of getting attention. It's unnerving to see things happening every day that have happened before, but this time the main characters are different and at least I've got a chance to stop them making the old mistakes.

Perhaps if I'd always insisted on Hayley and Karl having a share in the limelight cast on their eldest sister, I'd have stopped them from seeking attention in other ways, through drugs and crime. If I'd managed to get Janette to share her toys and treats with Neil, perhaps the two of them would have grown up good friends. And if I'd survived all the blows fate dealt me without turning to men and the bottle, perhaps I'd have known how to control the kids when they started to go off the rails. What I do know is that the four of them are so riddled with jealousy and resentment that nothing can now repair the damage. Karl married a Prestwich girl called Louise, but I'm afraid he's now serving another prison sentence for dealing in drugs and was inside when his son Kyle was born earlier this year. Hayley has been in one institution after another and needs psychiatric care. She keeps turning up on the doorstep and demanding to see Regan. On one visit she got hold of my photo-albums and destroyed all the pictures of me that she could find in them.

I'm fifty now and I've still got a lot to do with my life. I expect to have Regan to look after for a good few years yet, and how she turns out will show whether or not we really learn from our mistakes! I want to do something for myself as well. My life-plan at the moment is to lose some weight and to become an Aids counsellor. The first because that's what the hospital have told me I must do, and the second because I know from my own experience what it's like to need support and not to get it. I also want to start living again, and I don't mean clubbing and boozing. Nor do I mean settling down with a guy in marriage. George is the only man I look back on with affection but, in general, men have meant nothing but trouble in my life and I've become too much of my own person to hand over decisions to anyone else. I've spent so many years trying to please other people that if you'd asked me yesterday what I've ever done for Sheila Mottley I'd have had to say "Nothing", or at least "very little". But today all that's different because today I've finished writing this book. It's perhaps the only thing in my life that I can really call my own.